The Poin
An Introductio

John Molyneux

Bookmarks Publications

The Point is to Change it: An Introduction to Marxist Philosophy
John Molyneux

First published in 2012 by Bookmarks Publications
c/o 1 Bloomsbury Street, London WC1B 3QE

Typeset by Phil Whaite
Printed by Russell Press

ISBN 978 1 909026 01 8

Contents

About the author

John Molyneux is a socialist writer and activist, formerly a lecturer at Portsmouth University and now living in Dublin. His publications include *Marxism and the Party* (1978), *What is the Real Marxist Tradition?* (1985), *Rembrandt and Revolution* (2001), *Anarchism: A Marxist Criticism* (2011) and *Will the Revolution be Televised? A Marxist Analysis of the Media* (2011). He is a member of the Socialist Workers Party in Britain and Ireland.

Preface

The title of this small book comes, of course, from Marx. "Philosophers have only interpreted the world in various ways – the point, however, is to change it," the 11th and last of Marx's "Theses on Feuerbach", is inscribed on his grave in Highgate Cemetery, and rightly so. It sums up Marx's philosophy and it sums up the man. As Engels said, speaking at Marx's graveside:

> For Marx was before all else a revolutionist. His real mission in life was to contribute, in one way or another, to the overthrow of capitalist society and of the state institutions which it had brought into being, to contribute to the liberation of the modern proletariat, which he was the first to make conscious of its own position and its needs, conscious of the conditions of its emancipation. Fighting was his element. And he fought with a passion. (K Marx and F Engels, *Selected Works*, Vol 2, Moscow, 1962, p168)

The title also serves my purposes because what distinguishes this book from many of the introductions to Marxism already available is that, while it focuses on philosophy, it is written primarily for activists.

The last couple of years have seen the emergence, internationally, of a whole new generation of activists. From the Tunisian and Egyptian Revolutions and the rest of the Arab Spring to the *indignados* in Spain, the anti-austerity revolt in Greece, the Occupy movement in the US and many other struggles, big and small, round the world, people are taking to the streets in their millions. If this book reaches only a tiny fraction of those involved in this wave of revolt and is able to increase and clarify their understanding of Marxism, it will have achieved its main aim.

This aim has shaped the writing of this book in several ways. First, the language: I have tried to make the language, in contrast to most books on philosophy, as straightforward as possible. Clearly a work on Marxist philosophy cannot avoid talking about "dialectics" and "economic determinism" and the like, which are hardly everyday terms, but where such terms are used they are explained. My hope is that I have not oversimplified Marxist philosophy, but my priority has been accessibility to the reader who is new to the subject.

Second, the focus: I have focused on the way various aspects of Marxist philosophy are relevant to the struggle to change the world, rather than on the numerous debates in Marxist philosophy in the academic world. There is a chapter on Lukács, Gramsci and Althusser (which, the reader is warned, is unavoidably more difficult than the rest of the book) but I have concentrated on the philosophy of Marx and Engels, with inputs from Lenin and Trotsky – and not on Sartre, Adorno, Badiou and other "stars" of continental philosophy.

Third, the structure: I have included sections on alienation, exploitation and class struggle before moving onto more obviously "philosophical" areas, because I think a basic grasp of these concepts, which are widely misrepresented and misunderstood, is necessary for an understanding of the philosophy as a whole. Also I have devoted quite a lot of space to issues such as human nature, religion and morality, which do arise frequently in everyday life and in the movement. In general the level of argument tends to be as simple as possible at the beginning of the book and to increase in complexity as it goes along, together with the density of quotations and references. Sometimes the same issue, eg economic determinism, is returned to in more detail. This is in line with the attempt to achieve maximum accessibility.

One further point needs to be made at the outset. Mention Marx or Marxist philosophy and it is still the case that many, or maybe most, people think immediately of the Soviet Union under Stalin or Brezhnev and the other so-called "Communist" regimes in Eastern Europe, China, Cuba, North Korea, etc. These states are widely thought of as representing "Marxism in power", as "based on Marxism" or as "actually existing socialism", and this discredits both Marxism and socialism, because (a) they were undemocratic dictatorships and (b) they were largely rejected by their own people. I would also say that if these states did represent Marxism then many of Marxism's central claims would be refuted. For example it would not be the case that "the emancipation of the working class must be the act of the working class itself", nor would it be true that under socialism the state would start to wither away, or that racism or sexism would be overcome, and so on.

For my part I do not accept that any of these regimes (with the exception of the early years of the Russian Revolution) were Marxist or socialist in anything but name – rather I regard them as various versions of bureaucratic state capitalism, in which the state, engaged in competitive capital accumulation, exploits the working class. (This analysis of the Soviet Union is most fully developed in Tony Cliff's book *State Capitalism in Russia*.) This question impacts substantially on the subject matter of this book because the interpretation of Marxist philosophy I offer here is very different from the "official" version that prevailed in Stalinist Russia. For example, Soviet Marxism regarded the theme of alienation as something of a youthful aberration on Marx's part whereas I regard it as central to Marxism as a whole. Similarly Soviet Marxism held to a much more determinist interpretation of historical materialism than I offer here.

Thanks are due to Joseph Choonara and Paul Blackledge for useful comments on the manuscript, likewise to Grant Houldsworth for both technical assistance and many discussions on dialectics – we disagree but they have been helpful. And particular thanks to Sally Campbell at Bookmarks for all her work and assistance.

Finally, I want to dedicate this book to two people: to Mary Smith – everyone who knows me or knows Mary will understand why; and to the Marxist writer and activist, Chris Harman – everyone who knew Chris will understand that too.

John Molyneux
May 2012

1. Why philosophy matters

It is obvious that you do not have to know much about philosophy to participate in a demonstration, a strike or a revolutionary uprising. And a good job too. If we had to wait for large numbers of working people to read Marx and Hegel, demonstrations, strikes and, most certainly, revolutions would never happen.

However, the struggle for a better world does not consist only of these moments of direct confrontation. In between and during these "high points" there is a day-to-day battle of ideas, an ideological struggle against the worldview propagated by our rulers, and alongside this there is the day-to-day work of organisation, building and sustaining the union, the campaign or the political party. It is very difficult to sustain much ongoing political work for any length of time without a coherent alternative worldview to the dominant ideology which we encounter every day in the media (and at work, at school, at college, etc). A significant role in an alternative worldview is played by questions of philosophy.*

In the course of discussion with a friend or workmate they retort, "But there's one thing you've forgotten: you can't change human nature," or, "But there's always going to be rich and poor, always has been, always will be!" In a debate in the movement someone says, "The real problem is the Tories; we must all unite to get rid of them and get in Labour. Then things will be better." On a university sociology course the

* To attempt an exact definition of philosophy at this point would be a difficult and lengthy distraction. But what I mean by it in this book is, roughly, "general" or "abstract" thinking about human beings and their relations with society and nature.

professor says, "Of course Marx believed that communism was inevitable, but as social scientists we have to reject such dogmatic views," or, "Marxism reduces everything to economics and class, but sociology nowadays is more complex and sophisticated than that." All of these statements have an immediate plausibility – they seem to appeal to "common sense". This is because they rest on a worldview, a philosophy, systemically developed, perfected one might say, by our rulers, the capitalist class and its philosophical ideologists, over centuries and disseminated through innumerable channels to every corner of society. To answer them requires an equally developed and coherent philosophy from our side. Fortunately such a philosophy exists – Marxism.

Beyond the level of day-to-day debate and organisation, there is the question of leadership in the struggle: of participating in producing newspapers, journals, books; of deciding on the calling of demonstrations and strikes; of the tactics and strategy of campaigns and of parties and so on. The more an activist becomes involved in the direction and leadership of a campaign or movement, and especially at key turning points in the struggle, the more the coherence, breadth and depth of that activist's worldview is put to the test, the more questions of philosophy become important.

Let me give one concrete and very current example of the relevance of philosophy. The most widespread form of philosophy, especially as far as the mass of ordinary people are concerned, is religion. All religions include in their respective doctrines positions on important philosophical questions, such as the nature and meaning of human existence and the character of human nature ("ontology" or "the study of being" in academic philosophical terms), the source of knowledge and the criteria of truth (known as "epistemology"), and morality ("ethics"). Moreover, as a result particularly of the "War on Terror", the question of religion has moved to the centre of political debate.

The radical activist needs to be able to answer these arguments and respond to these positions and for this s/he needs a certain philosophical grounding. More than that s/he needs to know how to analyse and deal with religions and religious communities as social and political forces. This requires a *theoretical* understanding of the nature and development of religion. (An account of the Marxist position on religion appears later in this book.)

Another example is the problem faced by anyone or any organisation thinking of calling a demonstration, an occupation or a strike. This is the problem of judging the balance between the objective situation and the role of subjective initiative. Any campaigner or trade unionist who thinks that they can simply call demonstrations, occupations or strikes at will without regard for the circumstances will rapidly fall flat on their face. At the same time there are some people in the movement (especially certain kinds of trade union official) who always argue that the time is not right for struggle. This problem, which exists in embryo in every local campaign, becomes greatly magnified when the issue is a general strike, and can become literally a matter of life and death in a revolution. Learning to deal with this kind of problem is partly a matter of practical experience, but is greatly helped by a grasp of Marxist philosophy which is centrally concerned with how people "make their own history, but they do not make it just as they please; they do not make it under circumstances chosen by themselves" (K Marx, *The Eighteenth Brumaire of Louis Bonaparte*, in D McLellan, ed, *Karl Marx: Selected Writings*, Oxford, 1977, p300).

In short, philosophy and especially Marxist philosophy matters because it has an essential role to play in the struggle to change the world.

2. Where Marx's philosophy came from

Marx, with the assistance of his friend Frederick Engels, developed the main lines of his philosophy when he was very young, in his mid-twenties, and in a very short space of time between 1843 and 1846. It was a truly astonishing achievement. What made it possible?

Part of the answer, of course, is that he built on the work of other great philosophers and thinkers of his time and of the past. Most obviously he drew on and synthesised the tradition of German classical philosophy, above all G W F Hegel and his critic Ludwig Feuerbach*; the tradition of French political thought deriving from the French Revolution, particularly the so-called utopian socialists Fourier and Saint-Simon; and the classical political economy of Adam Smith and David Ricardo developed in Britain.

But while Marx openly acknowledged and paid tribute to all these influences he did not simply take over their ideas. Nor did he just draw them together. The new synthesis he created was based on a profound critique and transformation of his source materials. Thus from Smith and Ricardo he took the labour theory of value which stated that the value of commodities was determined by the amount of labour required in their production. But whereas for Smith and Ricardo this theory was used to support the "productive" industrial bourgeoisie against the "unproductive" landed aristocracy, Marx,

* G W F Hegel (1770-1831) was inspired by the French Revolution and developed a philosophical system which saw the whole of history as a dialectical development of ideas. Ludwig Feuerbach (1804-1872), a German philosopher of the next generation, developed a materialist critique of both religion and Hegel.

by applying it to the commodity of labour power, turned it into an exposure of the exploitation of the working class inherent in capitalist production. While for the utopian socialists, socialism was a noble rational ideal which they hoped to persuade the ruling class to accept, for Marx it was the necessary outcome of the working class's struggle for power. And, most importantly for our focus on philosophy, he took over dialectics from Hegel but, under the influence of Feuerbach, put it on a materialist foundation, while also transforming Feuerbach's rather passive materialism into a philosophy of human action. (The terms "materialism" and "dialectics" are explained in chapters 4 and 5.)

Marx was able to achieve this theoretical revolution not only because of his exceptional intellectual powers but also because he had discovered a new vantage point from which to examine all questions of philosophy and social theory – this was *the standpoint of the working class*.

Adopting the standpoint of the working class, which Marx did in 1843-44, meant much more than just sympathising with the plight of the workers (though there is much evidence in Marx's writing that he was deeply moved and outraged by the suffering of working people at the hands of the bourgeoisie). It meant grasping the power of the working class, its revolutionary potential to overthrow capitalism (see the section on class struggle in chapter 3). It meant seeing the working class not just as the agent, the foot soldiers, of the revolution but as its subject and directing element, in other words seeing the emancipation of the working class as the act of the working class itself. It meant understanding that in liberating itself the working class would also open the door to the liberation of humanity as a whole.

> All previous historical movements were movements of minorities, or in the interest of minorities. The proletarian

movement is the self-conscious, independent movement of the immense majority, in the interest of the immense majority. The proletariat, the lowest stratum of our present society, cannot stir, cannot raise itself up, without the whole superincumbent strata of official society being sprung into the air. (K Marx and F Engels, *The Communist Manifesto*, in D McLellan, ed, as above, p230)

It also meant that as a philosopher and as a theorist, Marx had to make the social position of the working class, its condition of life, its interests and its struggle the starting point for both his political programme and for his analysis of capitalism, history and philosophy. This Marx did, and this was why he repeatedly described himself and Engels as "theoreticians of the proletariat" (see for example, K Marx, *The Poverty of Philosophy*, in D McLellan, ed, as above, p212).

But Marx was only able to do this, to break with his middle class background and take the side of the working class, because the working class movement had already begun to make its appearance on the historical stage. For Marx as an individual three experiences were crucial. The first was mixing in communist worker circles in Paris in the second half of 1843. The second was the influence of Engels who had been working at his father's firm in Manchester and also reported to Marx on his involvement with the Chartists, the world's first independent mass workers' movement. The third was the revolt of the Silesian weavers who rose against their severe impoverishment in June 1844 and profoundly inspired Marx.

Thus it is no accident that Marxism was developed in the 1840s in north western Europe. This was where and when the industrial revolution was occurring and the modern working class was starting to flex its muscles. Marxism was the theoretical generalisation of working class struggle.

3. Alienation, exploitation and class struggle

The concepts in the title of this chapter are often treated as part of Marx's sociological or economic thought rather than his philosophy, but in reality Marxism is an integrated whole. I think they are so central to that whole that a brief treatment of them is necessary before moving on to discuss his more abstract philosophical theories such as materialism and dialectics.

Alienation

"Man is born free, and everywhere he is in chains," wrote the Enlightenment philosopher Jean-Jacques Rousseau. As the great radical poet William Blake noted in the London of the 1790s:

> I wander thro' each charter'd street,
> Near where the charter'd Thames does flow,
> And mark in every face I meet
> Marks of weakness, marks of woe.
> In every cry of every Man,
> In every Infant's cry of fear,
> In every voice, in every ban,
> The mind-forg'd manacles I hear.
> (William Blake, "London", 1794)

Observing similar symptoms philosophers of the time such as Hegel and Kierkegaard used the term "alienation" to describe the human condition. It meant that people were somehow "spiritually lost", were "estranged from their true selves" and suffered from "a loss of meaning in life". "Alienation" is still often used in this way today.

Marx, who saw the same symptoms, also used the term "alienation", especially in his early work *The Economic and Philosophical Manuscripts of 1844*. However, he produced an analysis of alienation that was both more precise and more down to earth, rooted in the material realities of people's actual lives, without losing any of its profundity and universal applicability.

For Marx alienation was rooted in people's relationship to the products of their labour and to their labour itself.

That workers are alienated from the products of their labour, ie are separated from them, and do not control them in any way, is a simple, obvious and observable fact – so obvious, so taken for granted, that it is normally not even commented on. It is just assumed, as if it were a law of nature, that when workers at Ford or Hyundai make cars, the cars belong to the company not to the workers; that when they dig coal or weave cloth the coal or the cloth belong to the owners of the mine or the mill. Marx, however, noticed it, questioned it, sought its origin and analysed its consequences. He saw that, "This fact simply implies that the object produced by labour, its product, now stands opposed to it as an *alien being*, as a *power independent* of the producer" (K Marx, *Early Writings*, London, 1963, p122).

Working people are dominated by the products of their own labour, and "the more the worker expends himself in work the more powerful becomes the world of objects which he creates in face of himself, the poorer he becomes in his newer life, and the less he belongs to himself" (as above, p122).

As a result:

> Labour certainly produces marvels for the rich but it produces privation for the worker. It produces palaces, but

hovels for the worker. It produces beauty, but deformity for the worker. (as above, p124)

In 2012 we can add that alienated labour has produced nuclear weapons capable of wiping out the human race and the likelihood of catastrophic climate change through the industrial generation of carbon emissions.

Marx then takes the analysis of alienation a stage further. He says that if workers are alienated from the *products* of their labour this can only be because they are alienated "in the *process of production*, within productive activity itself".

> The product is indeed only the *résumé* of the activity of production. Consequently, if the product of labour is alienation, production itself must be active alienation. The alienation of the object of labour merely summarises the alienation in the work activity itself. (as above, p124)

There has been a persistent tendency, especially among academic sociologists, to *reduce* what Marx is saying here to the observation that in industrial capitalism many workers' jobs are dirty, monotonous, boring, exhausting, dangerous, etc, or even further to the fact that many workers resent doing such boring, monotonous work – ie to reduce the concept of alienated labour to the physical conditions of work or a subjective feeling on the worker's part. This then leads to the view that alienation can be countered, or at least substantially alleviated, by making the work a bit more varied or interesting, or even with a new coat of paint on the factory walls or pumping out music over the tannoy. But Marx means much more than this. For Marx what is decisive is the social relationship of the worker to his or her work. It is the fact that the worker *sells* his or her ability to work to someone else (the employer/capitalist) and in doing so loses control over the purposes and methods of the work. The work is *for* someone else, not for him or herself, individually or collectively.

> What constitutes the alienation of labour? First, that the work is external to the worker, that it is not profit of his nature... His work is not voluntary but imposed, *forced labour*. It is not the satisfaction of a need, but only a *means* for satisfying other needs... The external character of work for the worker is shown by the fact that it is not his own work but work for someone else, that at work he does not belong to himself but to another person. (as above, pp124-125)

Wage labour, therefore, *is* alienated labour and the latter can be abolished only by abolishing wage labour, ie abolishing capitalism.

The fact that Marx locates the origin of alienation in the worker's relationship to work does not, however, make this a narrow economic concept, applicable only to the workplace. On the contrary, for Marx labour is fundamental to every aspect of human existence. In the first place Marx argues it was through labour that humans separated themselves from animals and became human. In the second place it is through labour that people shape their environment and themselves. Labour is the basis of history and society.

> Man can be distinguished from animals by consciousness, by religion or anything else you like. They themselves begin to distinguish themselves from animals as soon as they begin to produce their means of subsistence, a step which is conditioned by their physical organisation. By producing their means of subsistence men are indirectly producing their actual material life... This mode of production must not be considered simply as being the production of the physical

existence of the individuals. Rather it is a definite form of activity of these individuals, a definite form of expressing their life, a definite mode of life on their part. As individuals express their life, as they are. What they are, therefore coincides with their production, both with *what* they produce and *how* they produce. (K Marx and F Engels, *The German Ideology*, in D McLellan, ed, as above, pp160-161)

Because labour plays this fundamental role, the alienation of labour distorts the totality of human social relations. Marx analyses the consequences:

Since alienated labour: (1) alienates nature from men, and (2) alienates man from himself, from his own active function, his life activity, so it alienates him from the species… (3)… It alienates from man his own body, external nature, his mental life and his *human* life. (4) A direct consequence of the alienation of man from the product of his labour, from his life activity and from his species-life, is that *man is alienated* from other *men*. (K Marx, *Early Writings*, as above, pp127, 129.)

Examples of these different alienations abound in the contemporary world. Our alienation from nature is seen not only in climate change but also in the multitude of other ways in which capitalist industry pollutes and damages the environment (see, for example, John Bellamy Foster, Brett Clark and Richard York, *The Ecological Rift: Capitalism's War on the Earth*, New York, 2010). Our alienation from our bodies appears graphically in the phenomena of chronic obesity and anorexia, and the distorted, commodified forms of sexuality with which we are constantly bombarded in the media. Our alienation from other human beings is seen in widespread racism, xenophobia and scapegoating, promoted by our rulers but also accepted and internalised by sections of the working class.

Marx also relates alienation to the question of class. "If the product of labour does not belong to the worker...this can only be because it belongs to *a man other than the worker*" (K Marx, *Early Writings*, as above, p130). This "other man" is the capitalist "who does not work and is outside the work process" (as above, p131).

The capitalist and the worker, Marx argues, are two sides of the same coin of alienation, but there is a crucial difference:

> The propertied class and the class of the proletariat present the same human self-alienation. But the former class finds in this self-alienation its confirmation and its good, its own power: it has in it a semblance of human existence. The class of the proletariat feels annihilated in its self-alienation; it sees in it its own powerlessness and the reality of an inhuman existence... Within this antithesis the private property-owner is therefore the *conservative* side, the proletarian the *destructive* side. (K Marx, *The Holy Family*, in D McLellan, ed, as above, p134)

Alienated labour therefore produces an alienated society, an alienated world; a world out of control, a world of extremes of wealth and poverty, a world in which human beings are threatened by the products and consequences of their own work, estranged from each other as individuals and divided against each other by class and nation, by racism, sexism and religious hatred. A world in which everything from bread and water to sex, art, health and education are turned into commodities which thousands of millions cannot afford to buy.

In a word it produces our world today – a world that has to be changed if the human race is to survive and live free human lives.

Exploitation

Some commentators on Marx (most notably the French philosopher Louis Althusser, who I discuss in chapter 12) have claimed that the idea of alienation is present only in Marx's early writings and that he rapidly abandoned it in favour of the concept of exploitation. This is false. The theme of alienation and alienated labour appears throughout Marx's writing including his most important mature work, *Capital*. However, it is the case that Marx had to develop his theory of exploitation alongside the theory of alienation. This was because although alienation provided a profound general diagnosis of the ills of capitalism, a more precise quantifiable concept was needed to analyse the working of the capitalist economy, and the nature and dynamic of the class struggle.

In everyday language (which is heavily influenced by the ruling class) exploitation is a vague moral term used to condemn what is regarded as exceptionally bad behaviour by rogue bosses, for example, employers who pay wages below the socially accepted minimum. For Marx, however, exploitation has a precise scientific meaning – the systematic extraction of wealth by one group or class from the labour of another group or class – and exploitation is not the exception but the rule, inherent in the system, of every form of class society in history.

In pre-capitalist forms of class society – ancient slavery, feudalism, the state despotisms of India, China, etc – the exploitation of the slaves, serfs and peasants was fairly open and usually implemented by direct physical force. For example, the European serf of the Middle Ages was obliged either to work unpaid on the lord's land for, say, two days a week, or to give the lord, again unpaid, a portion of his produce. If the serf failed to comply, the lord's soldiers rapidly made an appearance.

But in capitalist society it appears on the surface – and certainly this is the view taken by the capitalists – that such exploitation has ceased. What they say is that the employer/employee relationship is a fair exchange, work for wages, freely entered into by both parties. Indeed they even expect the workers and society at large to be grateful to them for "creating jobs" and "providing work". And to the workers who have the temerity to complain or ask for more, they say, "No one is forcing you to work here, go and get a job elsewhere."

Marxism rejects this view completely. Capitalists do not create jobs or work. There was work before capitalism and there will be work after capitalism. Jobs are tasks that require performing, and arise from human needs. In the world today there are 7 billion people who need feeding, clothing, housing, educating, healing when they are sick, entertaining, transporting, etc. There is thus an abundance of work for these same 7 billion people to do. What capitalists actually do, through their ownership and control of the means of production, is make it impossible for the majority of human beings to work except by working for them. Nor, of course, do they employ people as a charitable exercise but in order to make profit, ie to expand the value of their capital, and the workers enter into the wage contract not "freely" but because it is the only way they can earn a living.

Most importantly Marx demonstrated that within the wage-labour relationship there lay concealed unpaid labour just as real as the unpaid labour of the serf. The starting point of this demonstration is Marx's understanding that under capitalism workers' labour power (their ability to work) is sold as a commodity like every other commodity. The value of a commodity (value is not the same as price, but is the underlying point around which prices oscillate) is determined, Marx says, by the amount of socially necessary labour time required to produce it. The reason a loaf of bread sells for £1 while a shirt sells for £20 and a car for £10,000 is, in the final analysis, that it takes 10,000 times as many hours of labour to make a car, and 20 times as many to make a shirt, as it does to make a loaf of bread.*

Apply this to labour power and it follows that the value of labour power, ie the wage it is paid, is determined by the amount of labour time socially necessary to produce it, ie feed, clothe, train the worker so that s/he is able to work.

However, in one vital respect human labour power differs from all other commodities: it is attached to a living person and is creative. Human labour power can produce more value than it costs to reproduce the labour power itself. This difference, this "surplus value" as Marx called it, is pocketed by the capitalist and is the source of the capitalist's profit. What it means is that the worker who works, say, eight hours a day, 40 hours a week and is paid say £80 a day, £400 a

---

* There are two key arguments which demonstrate the truth of this labour theory of value. The first is that there exist an infinite number of commodities, with an infinite variety of qualities (weight, size, shape, colour, smell, taste, durability, etc) serving an infinite variety of human purposes: one quality all commodities have in common and which alone can serve as a measure of their relative value, ie determine the proportions in which they exchange with either, is that they embody a definite amount of necessary labour time. The second is that this law of value is enforced by capitalist competition: if capitalist A consistently sells his products below their value (their cost of production) he will make a loss and will go out of business. If capitalist A consistently sells his products above their value, capitalist B (or C or D) will, sooner or later, be able to undercut him and he will again go out of business. In the long run, therefore, competition obliges rival capitalists to sell their commodities at prices which fluctuate around their value measured in labour time.

week, produces the goods or services equal to their wages in say, five hours of the day or 25 hours of the week and in reality works three hours a day, 15 hours a week, unpaid.

If this were not the case, if capitalists did not extract surplus value and make a profit out of workers' labour, they would have no reason to employ them. And when they cease to make a profit out of the labour of the workers they employ, they promptly "let them go", ie sack them.

Marx's theory of surplus value is of enormous significance. It exposes the ideological, self-serving nature of the capitalist view of wage labour, but it does much more than this. It enables the rate of exploitation/surplus value to be calculated and expressed mathematically and the same for the rate of profit – surplus value as a proportion of the capitalist's total outlay on wages, raw materials and fixed capital. In Marx's formula: $R=S/(C+V)$ (where R = rate of profit, S = surplus value, C = constant capital, ie machines, buildings, raw materials, etc, and V = variable capital, ie wages).

The rate of profit is the fundamental factor determining the level of capitalist investment, the level of employment and the rate of growth or contraction, ie the general health or sickness, of the capitalist economy. The law of the tendency of the rate of profit to decline outlined by Marx in *Capital*, Volume 3, is the principal contradiction underlying capitalism's tendency to economic crisis (this is explained in chapter 6 below). The theory of surplus value is thus the cornerstone of Marx's whole critical analysis of capitalist production.

However, the theory of surplus value does something else as well: it shows that at the heart of capitalist production, and therefore of capitalist society, lies a direct and irreconcilable conflict of interest. The longer the working day the greater the proportion of unpaid labour and of surplus value there will be for the capitalist; the shorter the working day the lower the proportion of unpaid labour; the lower the level of wages the higher the level of profit; the higher the wages the lower the profits. Profits and wages, Marx says:

> stand in inverse ratio to each other. Capital's exchange value, profit, rises in the same proportion as labour's share, wages, falls and vice versa. Profit rises to the extent that wages fall; it falls to the extent that wages rise... The interests of capital and the interests of wage labour are diametrically opposed. (K Marx, *Wage Labour and Capital*, in D McLellan, ed, as above, pp261-62.)

Thus Marx's theory of exploitation, his theory of surplus value, leads directly to the theory of class and class struggle.

Class struggle

There is probably no concept more closely associated with Marx and Marxism than class, but there is also no concept so widely misunderstood. Confusion about class reigns at every level: in the media, in everyday life and in the academic world.

One of the most common confusions is the notion that class is primarily a matter of people's social origins, of their position at birth, and of inherited privilege or disadvantage. This is basically a hangover from the bourgeoisie's struggle against feudalism, when the bourgeoisie championed "equality" (of legal rights and opportunity) against the inherited privileges and power of the feudal aristocracy. It is this view that leads to the utterly mistaken idea that class is disappearing or becoming less important in modern society (or that America, because it was never feudal and had no aristocracy, is somehow a classless society). Of course it is true that inherited privilege and wealth still play an important role in modern capitalism (just look at the role of Old Etonians in the British ruling class) but it is not the heart of the matter either for Marxist theory or in actual social practice. It is current social position not social origin that is crucial. The child of working class parents who becomes a manager or boss, behaves as a manager or boss not as a worker. The young black kid who grows up to become president of the United States behaves as the political representative of US imperialism not the representative of black people.

Another widespread confusion is that class is primarily about income and/or lifestyle. Obviously class plays a major role in determining income and lifestyle, but neither income nor lifestyle determines class. Inequalities of wealth and lifestyle, however wide they may be, nevertheless form a continuum from top to bottom and therefore cannot yield a coherent analysis of the class structure. On the basis of income or lifestyle one could conclude that there are five, ten or 15 classes, or none, and either way it is arbitrary. Moreover, individuals might have the same income and be members of different classes, eg a skilled manual worker and the owner of a small corner shop, or be members of the same class and live very different lifestyles.

In sociology, the academic discipline that deals with class, class is usually defined in terms of different life chances (opportunities for obtaining goods and services, for educational achievement, for getting a good job, for living a healthy and long life, etc) and the Marxist theory of class is dealt with roughly as follows:

For Marx, they say, class is defined by "relationship to the means of production", leading to a two-class model of society consisting of a property-owning capitalist class or bourgeoisie, and propertyless working class or proletariat. There was some truth in this, but it is too simple; for the analysis of modern society a more complex model is required and this is provided by Max Weber and his latter-day disciples. For Weber class is not just a matter of property ownership or lack of it but of position in the labour market. Between the capitalists and the (manual) workers there is a middle class based on the mental skills and educational qualifications that they bring to the job market. As capitalism becomes technologically more sophisticated this class grows while the working class shrinks. Class polarisation fails to materialise. Moreover there are many other divisions in society based on "status" – contemporary Weberians would cite particularly gender and ethnicity – which cut across class and are often more important than class in determining people's identity, and which Marx and Marxists have neglected.

This is a false account of Marx's theory of class in many respects. Marx didn't have a simple two-class model and was well aware of the existence of intermediate layers, the so-called middle class, and paid a good deal more attention to gender and race issues than Weber ever did – but this is not the key point. The key point is that at the heart of the Marxist theory of class are not unequal life chances (important as they are) but exploitation, the extraction of surplus value discussed in the last section. It is the daily fact of exploitation, the conflict of interest inherent in capitalist social relations, that produces the capitalists and workers as antagonistic classes.

The capitalists are those whose survival (as capitalists) depends on profit, which derives from the surplus value obtained from wage labour. The workers are those whose survival depends on the wages they receive for the sale of their labour power to the capitalist. This relationship locks the former and the latter into perpetual combat. Whether the capitalist inherited or built up his or her capital, went to public school or was born on a council estate, and whether the worker earns high wages or low, works in an office or school or a factory, or expends principally mental or physical energy, this does not change the essential conflict of interest.

The conflict of interest which has its source at the point of production extends, like the alienation which it parallels, throughout the society based on this production. It becomes a conflict of interest, a class conflict, in every issue of state and public policy from taxation to health services to crime and punishment, to foreign policy, arms spending, war and the preservation of the environment.

Neither Weber nor his sociological heirs, nor the journalists, nor the media commentators, grasp this at all and consequently their criticism of Marx misses its mark completely.

The middle classes, of which they make so much, certainly exist but their position is determined neither by their status nor by their lifestyle (both of which are consequences not causes of class position), but by their role in the processes of exploitation and class conflict.

Between the bourgeoisie (the capitalist class) and the proletariat (the working class) there are two quite large social groups. The first is the owners of small businesses, the petty bourgeoisie, whose typical representative is the small shopkeeper. This layer is oppressed by big business and even to some extent exploited (via finance capital and the banks) but it is also, and crucially, an exploiter of wage labour on a small scale. The second group consists of managers who are paid employees but whose function is to oversee the extraction of surplus value from the workers. For example, the manager of a supermarket is paid a wage but that wage is not for stacking shelves or serving customers, but for ensuring that the workers do this "efficiently" – ie in such a way that the employer makes as much profit as possible – and that wage is generally considerably higher than the wages of the workers so as to ensure the manager's loyalty.

This "middle class" is not really a distinct class; rather it is a hierarchy of intermediate strata whose social role combines (in different proportions at different levels) elements of the capitalist and elements of the proletarian condition. At its upper end the middle class merges into the ruling class (senior corporation managers, senior civil servants and police chiefs are examples) and at its lower end (the self-employed plumber or painter and decorator or lower line manager) it merges into the proletariat. In the struggle between the capitalist class and the working class the middle class vacillates according to the strength of the gravitational pull of the two fundamental classes.

The different understandings of class in the Marxist and the Weberian or "common sense" perspectives lead to dramatically different pictures of the class structure in modern capitalism. Marx was emphatic that, "In proportion as the bourgeoisie, ie capital, is developed, in the same proportion is the proletariat, the modern working class developed" and that "the proletarian movement is...the movement of the immense majority in the interest of the immense majority" (K Marx and F Engels, *The Communist Manifesto*, in D McLellan, ed, as above, pp226, 230).

By contrast in the Weberian/common sense view the development of capitalism leads to a decline of the proletariat as a proportion of the population. The issue cannot be resolved simply by counting heads because it is really a dispute about which heads to count. For the Weberians the proletariat consists only of "industrial" or "manual" workers (these terms are in themselves problematic – doesn't a programmer work with his or her hands, doesn't an electrician use his or her brain?) who are indeed shrinking in numbers in the developed capitalist countries, while the "white collar" or "non-manual" employees, seen as middle class, expand.

From the Marxist standpoint, however, the majority of, though not all, white collar employees (teachers, social workers, civil servants, secretaries, shop workers, nurses, etc) live by the sale of their labour power and are exploited by capitalists. The exploitation of some white collar workers, such as teachers and health workers in the public sector, is less easy to see than that of workers who produce commodities in private industry, but what they are really doing is producing and reproducing the commodity of labour power for the capitalist system, and like other workers they are paid less than the value of what they produce. They are therefore part of the working class and, in practice, act as such. The PCS (civil servants' union) and the NUT (National Union of Teachers) have been in the forefront of the recent struggles over pension rights in Britain, while teachers and tax collectors have played an important role in the ongoing Egyptian Revolution. Once this is grasped it is clear that the working class or proletariat continues to constitute the large majority of the population in the developed capitalist countries, approximately 70 percent or more, and is on its way to becoming the most numerous class in the world as a whole.

It is interesting to note that whereas for most of the bourgeois views of class the division between the working class and the middle class is seen as a division between occupations (eg miners and teachers) for Marxists the dividing line runs *within* occupations. Thus most teachers are workers but head teachers are managers, most social workers are workers but (in Britain) team managers and above are becoming middle class. In the civil service the lower ranks are working class, but the topmost ranks are more or less part of the ruling class. It is also interesting that, whereas most academic sociologists ignore or fail to consider these distinctions, workers, especially trade unionists, who actually do these jobs, are acutely aware of them.

However, for Marx the most important feature of his theory of class was his identification of the working class's revolutionary role. There were three elements to this. First, the working class conflict of interest with the capitalist class (which I have already outlined); second, its power; third, its ability to create a classless society. The power of the working class derives from the fact that its labour is the main producer of wealth and profit in society, from the dependence of all systems of transport, energy production, communications and state operations on its labour, and from its concentration in large numbers in workplaces and cities. This power gives the working class the capacity to defeat the bourgeoisie and its state. Its capacity to create a classless society derives from the necessarily collective nature of its struggle (from the smallest local dispute to the widest general strike and insurrection), from the fact that it can only take possession of the means of production collectively, and from its potential, unlike any previous class in history, to be both the producing and ruling class in society at the same time, thus ending the very basis of class division.

The revolutionary role of the working class is the core doctrine of Marxism both politically *and* philosophically.* Politically it is central because Marxism is indeed about changing the world and if the working class does not have the capacity to become revolutionary capitalism cannot be overthrown and socialism cannot be achieved – unless, of course, socialism could be brought about by parliamentary reform or alternatively imposed by a coup or conspiracy from above, in which case Marxism would be fundamentally refuted and redundant. Philosophically it is central because the struggle of the working class is the material basis on which Marxism arose, and "the standpoint of the working class" is the vantage point from which he developed all his main theories including the labour theory of

---

* "The chief thing in the doctrine of Marx is that it brings out the historic role of the proletariat as the builder of socialist society" – V I Lenin, *Collected Works*, Vol 18, Moscow, 1975, p582.

value and historical materialism. This idea is returned to and elaborated at various stages in this book.*

However, it is also probably the most criticised and rejected aspect of Marxism, not only by pro-capitalist sociologists, Weberians, liberals and social democrats but also by radical intellectuals, "academic" Marxists and so on. At various points between the 1950s and the 1980s the revolutionary role of the proletariat was rejected by left sociologists such as C Wright Mills, John Rex, Ralf Dahrendorf, Tom Bottomore and Anthony Giddens; the Frankfurt School philosophers such as T W Adorno, Herbert Marcuse and Jürgen Habermas; the theorists of revolt in the Third World such as Frantz Fanon and Régis Debray; the American Marxist economists Paul Baran and Paul Sweezy; the French philosopher André Gorz (who, in 1980, wrote *Farewell to the Proletariat*, the classic text of this genre); the communist historian Eric Hobsbawm, and many others. Indeed there were times when there seemed to be something close to intellectual consensus on this question. The main exceptions were those leftists influenced by Maoism who were quite a force in the 1960s and early 1970s (but whose commitment to "the proletariat" tended to be abstract and rhetorical rather than actual: at the heart of Maoism was the idea of a party or "leadership" acting *on behalf of* the proletariat) and the Trotskyists of various kinds who attempted to build working class revolutionary parties.

Nevertheless in this period major working class struggles continued to occur, such as the big industrial battles in Britain in the early 1970s and the Italian "hot autumn" of 1969, sometimes reaching pre-revolutionary proportions as

* The relationship between the social being of the proletariat and the development of Marxist theory is also explored in J Molyneux, *What is the Real Marxist Tradition?*, London, 1985.

in the French general strike in May 1968, Chile in 1972-73, the Portuguese Revolution of 1974, the Iranian Revolution of 1979 and Poland in 1980-81 (for analysis of these events see C Barker, ed, *Revolutionary Rehearsals*, London, 1987).

The rise of the international anti-capitalist movement following the Seattle demonstration of 1999 has produced a new layer of radical theorists and philosophers some of whom have achieved a kind of "intellectual star status" and a wide readership for their work: Michael Hardt and Antonio Negri, Naomi Klein, John Holloway, David Harvey, Slavoj Žižek, Alain Badiou and Terry Eagleton are names that spring to mind. Most of these theorists (Eagleton is an exception) also reject the centrality of the working class. Most importantly Hardt and Negri, in their influential books *Empire* and *Multitude*, argue that "the multitude" has replaced the working class as the revolutionary subject for our times. This and related ideas have certainly had a resonance in the recent *indignados* and Occupy movements. I will discuss these issues, along with some other critiques of the concept of the working class, in an appendix at the end of this book.

Here two points need to be made. First, that the modern working class, defined as those who live only by the sale of their labour power, far from disappearing, has never been as numerous as it is today. In 2002 Chris Harman, in a careful analysis based on Dean Filmer's 1995 report for the World Bank, *Estimating the World at Work*, concluded that "the worldwide total figure for the working class comes to between 1.5 and 2 billion" and commented, "Anyone who believes we have said 'farewell' to this class is not living in the real world" (C Harman, "The Workers of the World", *International Socialism* 96 (autumn 2002), p6). Since then the size of the international working class has increased substantially, not least because of the massive economic growth in China and India. Minqi Li writes:

> Nonagricultural employment, as a share of China's total employment, increased from 31 percent in 1980 to 50 percent in 2000, and increased further to 60 percent in 2008. According to a report prepared by the Chinese Academy of Social Sciences in 2002, about 80 percent of the nonagricultural labour force consisted of proletarianised wage workers, such as industrial workers, service workers, clerical workers, and the unemployed. Since the overwhelming majority of nonagricultural workers are wage workers who have to sell their labour power to make a living, the rapid growth of nonagricultural employment suggests massive formations of the proletarianised working class in China. (http://monthlyreview.org/2011/06/01/the-rise-of-the-working-class-and-the-future-of-the-chinese-revolution)

Urbanisation is not the same as proletarianisation but it is closely connected and the fact that the proportion of the world's population living in cities passed the 50 percent mark in 2010, as compared to 37 percent in 1970, can only mean a big growth in the working class. The only way this can be denied is if the working class is equated solely with the traditional industrial working class – a view I have already argued against.

Secondly, this working class, especially in the last two years, is showing strong signs of combativity in many countries. In the Tunisian Revolution of 2010-11 the working class and the main trade union federation played a leading role in the overthrow of the dictator, Ben Ali, and likewise it was the combination of massive street mobilisations (involving huge numbers of workers) and workers' strikes that drove out Mubarak in Egypt. In Greece and Spain there have been multiple general strikes and major confrontations in the streets. In China there has been a considerable wave of strikes and working class protest, and even in Britain 2011 saw a mass trade union demonstration of over half a million in March, followed by a mass strike of more than 2 million on 30 November.

In other words, there are no grounds for abandoning Marx's view that the working class is the principal agent of socialist change.

4. Materialism

Marx's philosophy as a whole is commonly known as "dialectical materialism". The validity of this term has been contested on the grounds that Marx himself did not use it and that it was widely used by Stalinism (in a very dogmatic and mechanical fashion). Nevertheless, to me "dialectical materialism" seems a reasonable description and one thing is clear: Marx's philosophy was materialist and was dialectical. For the purposes of this introduction I shall discuss these terms in turn.

In everyday language "materialist" means greedy or personally acquisitive, as opposed to "idealist" which means holding ideals. In this sense, Marx, who lived most of his life in dire poverty, was clearly an idealist, not a materialist. But the philosophical meaning of materialist and idealist is quite different. Here the issue is the relationship between mind and matter, between ideas and material conditions – which is to be considered primary in shaping human history? Philosophical idealists, from Plato to Hegel, give priority to mind and ideas. Philosophical materialists, from Democritus to Ludwig Feuerbach, give priority to matter. Marx and Marxist philosophy stand firmly in the materialist camp.

Materialism in philosophy involves commitment to the following propositions:

- The material world exists.
- The material world exists independently of human consciousness.
- Real, if not total and absolute, knowledge of the world is possible.
- Human beings are part of nature, albeit a distinct part.

– The material world does not derive from human thought; human thought derives from the material world.

The first three of these propositions are, of course, a kind of common sense, but they are common sense because they are confirmed by human practice millions or billions of times every day. Indeed it is impossible to live daily life on other than materialist assumptions. The eminent idealist philosopher can imagine that the world does not exist, or exists outside of human ken, but s/he cannot make breakfast, board a bus, walk across a bridge or carry out a thousand everyday tasks on any but a materialist basis. Likewise more or less the whole of modern science, equally confirmed in practice on a daily basis, is built on materialist premises. For Marx this test of practice was decisive.

> The question whether objective truth can be attributed to human thinking is not a question of theory but is a practical question. In practice man must prove the truth ie the reality and power, the this-sidedness of his thinking. The dispute over the reality or non-reality of thinking which is isolated from practice is a purely scholastic question. (K Marx, "Theses on Feuerbach", www.marxists.org/archive/marx/works/1845/theses/theses.htm)

The fourth proposition is in accordance with, and confirmed by, the findings of modern science, in particular by Darwin's theory of evolution, by genetics (humans share 98 percent of their DNA sequence with chimpanzees) and by the fossil record (such as the 6 million year old *Orrorin tugenensis* fossils found in Kenya in 2000 or the *Australopithecus afarensis* from between 3.9 and 2.9 million years ago).

The fifth proposition follows from the previous four, but is also the most distinctively Marxist. Prior to Marx almost all accounts of human history were top down, taking as their starting point the deeds and ideas of great men.

It is common to find people who are more or less automatically materialists with regards to propositions one to four, ie the relations between humans and nature, but who adopt an idealist standpoint when it comes to dealing with society, history and politics. They say or write things like "US foreign policy is based on the idea that America has a God-given right to lead the world", or that "capitalism is driven by a belief in economic growth", or that "the Cold War was fundamentally a clash of ideologies". In other words they hold that the analysis of society and history begins with the ideas, beliefs and values in people's heads, and that it is their conceptions which explain the nature of the economy, the social structure and the behaviour of governments.

This contradiction is not an accident; it reflects the influence of bourgeois ideology. For its struggle against feudalism, for the development of capitalist industry, and also for its numerous military operations the bourgeoisie needed a rapid development of science, which was dependent on a materialist view of nature. But for the maintenance and justification of its social position the bourgeoisie needs an idealist view of history and society – a view that makes its point of departure the ideas and actions of outstanding individuals, usually members and representatives of the ruling classes.

In contrast the working class – and revolutionary socialists – need a genuinely scientific analysis of society so as to be able to change it. They need to know what are the driving forces and material interests that underlie the policies of politicians. They need a materialist analysis that makes not the ideas of great men but first the daily labour and deeds of the mass of ordinary working people, and second the interests of ruling classes, the starting point for its account of history.

Marx summed up his materialist viewpoint in the phrase,

"It is not consciousness that determines social being, but social being that determines social consciousness" (K Marx, Preface to *A Contribution to the Critique of Political Economy*, in D McLellan, ed, as above, p389). The precise meaning of this phrase is best explained and grasped by means of some historical examples.

The first example I would give is the period of European history known as the Reformation, normally thought of as being instigated by Martin Luther, when he nailed his 95 theses (attacking church corruption) to the door of the Castle Church in Wittenberg on 31 October 1517. The Reformation brought about a schism in the formally universal (in western Europe) church between Catholics and Protestants (with further subdivisions emerging) which plunged Europe into an era of upheaval, revolution and war lasting almost 200 years.

Mainstream history takes this great conflict as essentially a religious struggle, ie a struggle between people with different beliefs about god, the church and the Bible. In other words it adopts an idealist interpretation. In contrast Marxism sees the Reformation as fundamentally the ideological expression of the class struggle between the rising bourgeoisie and the old feudal aristocracy and of the transition from the feudal to the capitalist mode of production. In other words Marxism offers a materialist interpretation.

The debate between the two positions is given particular focus by the German sociologist Max Weber's famous work of 1904, *The Protestant Ethic and the Spirit of Capitalism*. Weber argued that Protestantism encouraged an ethic of hard work, saving and reinvestment by its teaching that success in business was evidence of being in receipt of God's grace, and that was necessary to establish the habits required for capitalism to get off the ground. This recognised the link between Protestantism and capitalism, but made Protestant theology and morality the major causal factor in the development of capitalism, whereas Marxism views the embryonic emergence of capitalist production, at first within the framework of feudalism, as producing the ideological phenomenon of Protestantism. This was not only because Protestantism encouraged hard work but because the Catholic Church was both materially, in terms of massive land ownership, and ideologically, in terms of its insistence on subservience to the church hierarchy, tied to the feudal aristocracy and the feudal system. In order to challenge that system the bourgeoisie needed an ideological alternative to Catholicism.

Since Marxist materialism is repeatedly attacked by the method of oversimplifying and caricaturing it to the point where it is obviously false, it is worth saying briefly what the materialist view does not claim or imply. It does not claim or imply that the historical actors of the time were cynical or not sincere in their religious beliefs, or that they consciously adopted those beliefs as a deliberate cloak for their material interests. Of course some individuals may have done this, but this is not the point of the theory, which is rather to explain how real material conditions and interests led masses of people to be drawn, sincerely, to religious doctrines that fitted their circumstances and seemed to articulate their needs. Nor does the materialist view imply any mechanical one-to-one relationship between class and religion – it does not claim that all feudal lords and rulers were Catholics and all burghers or early bourgeois were Protestants, still less that all Catholics were lords and all Protestants were bourgeois, and is therefore not refuted by the fact that this was not so. All the Marxist materialist view asserts is that amid and through all the immense complexity of real historical processes the economic development and class interests are the underlying driving force.

The great weakness of all idealist interpretations is that

they are unable to offer a rational explanation of the historical emergence of the ideas to which they give primacy – they are simply left hanging arbitrarily in the air or explained as a result of previous ideas which in turn are left hanging.

My second example is the rise of imperialism and racism. The close of the 15th century saw the beginning of a long historical process in which the major European powers (and later the US) came to dominate the rest of the world – North America, Latin America, Africa, Asia, the Middle East, Australasia, Polynesia, etc. This process involved slavery and the slave trade, colonial conquest and rule and the exercise of international economic and military power. It was accompanied by innumerable atrocities, systematic exploitation, oppression and degradation of the subordinated peoples and a no less systematic international ideology of racism which affirmed the inherent inferiority of non-European (non-white) peoples. Idealist commentators on this history, the most subtle and sophisticated of whom is probably Edward Said, author of the famous *Orientalism*, assert that the driving force behind this vast conquest was the pre-existing Eurocentric and racist mindset of Christian Europe – the so-called "West". The Marxist materialist view argues rather that it was the logic of capitalism – the competitive struggle for raw materials, cheap labour and markets, all for the purpose of profit and capital accumulation – that drove the whole process. Racism and Eurocentrism were its ideological reflection and justification, especially in regard to the Atlantic slave trade and slavery in the Americas. (The Marxist analysis of racism is discussed further in chapter 9.)

A third example is the question of war. Wars are commonly fought in the name of high-sounding principles – freedom, democracy, national self-defence, the right of nations to self-determination and so on. This is particularly true at the moment with the notion of "humanitarian intervention" regularly deployed by US presidents and British prime ministers. Marxist materialism rejects this and maintains that wars are, almost invariably, fought for real material interests – the interests of the regimes and ruling classes that instigate them.* These interests may be the direct acquisition of land or raw materials (water, oil, diamonds, etc) or access to markets and cheap labour but they may also be broader strategic interests. For example the US invaded Afghanistan not primarily for any resources in that ravaged and impoverished country (nor, of course, to free the Afghan people from the tyranny of the Taliban or to liberate Afghan women!) but as part of its overall strategy for the defence of the (informal) US empire, which included both inflicting exemplary punishment for 9/11 and gaining control of central Asia as a hedge against future Chinese power. Similarly the NATO intervention against Gaddafi in Libya, under cover of saving the people from a massacre, was really motivated by both getting control of Libyan oil and the need to halt the revolutionary dynamic of the Arab Spring which threatened Western dominance of the Middle East. Strategic interests may not be immediately economic but they are economic one or two steps down the line.

Marxist philosophy is materialist: it insists on the primacy of matter over mind in general and the primacy of the material production of the necessities of life in explaining history. However, there are different versions of materialism and Marx's was significantly different from the materialism that prevailed before he came on the scene, namely that of the

* It is worth saying that very, very few wars actually arise from popular pressure and those that do are generally wars of colonial liberation or civil wars, ie revolutions. Wars are normally launched by rulers and in so far as they are accompanied by pro-war popular sentiment this is because it is deliberately whipped up in favour of a war that has already been decided on at the top.

18th century Enlightenment. That materialism was associated with the rising bourgeoisie and took a mechanistic view of human behaviour, which was seen as shaped by external conditions with little or no focus on the active role of humans in making history. The way in which Marx's materialism developed beyond this will be explored in the next chapter and at various points in the rest of this book.

5. Dialectics

As we have already noted Marx was by no means the first materialist, but he *was* the first *dialectical* materialist. This signifies that for Marx, while historical development was driven by material forces and interests rather than ideas, the process of change was not smooth, gradual, mechanical or automatic.

The term "dialectic" originates in ancient Greek philosophy where it meant the idea of arriving at the truth through debate or dialogue. Marx, however, took dialectics from the great German philosopher Hegel who, inspired by the French Revolution, had developed a comprehensive philosophical system in which the whole of world history was seen as an ascending succession of conflicting ideas.

Dialectics has a fearsome reputation. Of all Marx's key ideas dialectics is the one most often thought of as being obscure, difficult or even mysterious. There are several reasons for this: because the word itself is not in common usage; because it isn't taught in school or even university; because it is associated with Hegel who *is* very difficult; and most importantly, because it contradicts what, for centuries, has been represented as common sense or obvious. Nevertheless, I want to insist that the basic ideas of dialectics are *not* that difficult. They are well within the reach of any thinking worker or activist. Anyone who has followed the main ideas of this book so far will be able to follow this section too.

I have already said that for dialectical materialism the process of change involved contradictions and the conflict of opposing forces. To understand dialectics further we need to unpack this statement. Let us start with the question of change. At the heart of dialectics is the proposition that everything changes. "Everything" here refers to everything in the universe from the totality of the universe itself to the tiniest particle. For a start everything is in motion, the most basic form of change, but everything is also developing, altering, evolving, coming into being or passing out of being. As Bob Dylan once put it, "Who isn't busy being born, is busy dying."

This fundamental principle of dialectics is entirely in accord with, and confirmed by all the findings of modern science from Copernicus, through Kepler, Newton, Darwin, and Einstein to quantum mechanics and big bang theory. In other words, it is a well established fact.

However, it is a fact which has very revolutionary political implications. It means that every existing regime, every existing social order no matter how apparently powerful and secure is destined to disappear. Now, after the fall of the Bourbons and the Romanovs in the French and Russian Revolutions, the idea that all political regimes are, sooner or later, doomed to extinction may be quite commonplace, but it remains a central theme of bourgeois ideology that bourgeois social relations, ie capitalism, are eternal – capitalism will survive forever, no alternative is possible. Hence the liberating quality of the slogan "Another world is possible". As a university teacher I tried to encourage free discussion in my classes but I had a half-serious rule that students were not allowed to say that anything would *always* be so. Interestingly they found this very hard to observe. They kept wanting to say things such as "There will always be a certain amount of racism" or "Women will never be totally equal" or "There will always be rich and poor" for the simple reason that they had been fed these messages, explicitly or implicitly, since birth. In contrast dialectics insists that nothing lasts forever, and that everything, day by day, second by second, is involved in a process of constant change.

But, of course, constant change is only one side of the

story. As well as change there is continuity. The sun rose yesterday and will rise tomorrow, as it has done for billions of years. Women have not "always" been oppressed but they have been oppressed for a very long time and remain oppressed today. We know that in the fullness of time mountains rise and fall and continents change shape but from the standpoint of one human generation or even most of human history they remain largely the same. Capitalism is constantly changing in a multitude of ways but its central drive, the competitive accumulation of capital, persists over centuries. Indeed for the purposes of everyday life the element of continuity is frequently more important than the element of change and the history of human thought has reflected this.

Modern science may show that everything is changing, but for millennia the dominant approach was to recognise change but to see it only in relation to a fixed and unchanging background. The sun and stars moved in the heavens, but on fixed paths around an unmoving earth, the still centre of the cosmos. Animals and people lived and died but the species, created by God, remained immutable. Above all there was held to be a permanent unchangeable human nature.

Also human knowledge, and this applies both to humanity as a whole and to individuals, tends to begin with distinguishing between "things" and identifying their different characteristics – this is summer, this is winter; this berry is edible, this one is poisonous; this animal is a dog, this is a cat; this animal is wild and dangerous, this one is tameable; this is my mother, this is my father; this is my brother, this is my friend. Along with these necessary distinctions went a search for regularities, recurring patterns which were thought of as "laws" of nature, such as Newton's first law of motion (that the velocity of a body remains constant unless the body is acted upon by an external force) or Boyle's law (for a fixed amount of an ideal gas kept at a fixed temperature, pressure and volume are inversely proportional – if one doubles, the other halves).

Accompanying the development of practical human knowledge and science along these lines, there was also developed (by Aristotle and his successors) a system of logic, ie rules of sound thinking. Logic was meant to tell you whether or not what you were saying, writing or thinking made sense. A proposition that was logical was not necessarily true (in fact), but it had the possibility of being true. A proposition that was not logical, ie broke the rules of logic, could not possibly be true. The basic principles of this Aristotelian or formal logic were the "law of identity" and "the law of non-contradiction". The "law of identity" stated, in symbolic terms, that A is equal to A, or an ounce of gold equals an ounce of gold, or, taking a unique object to make it absolutely clear, Leonardo da Vinci's *Mona Lisa* is equal to Leonardo da Vinci's *Mona Lisa*. The "law of non-contradiction" stated that A cannot be equal to non-A, ie it makes no sense to say that an ounce of gold is not an ounce of gold or the *Mona Lisa* is not the *Mona Lisa*. On the basis of these apparently "obvious" propositions a system of logic or sound reasoning was erected, exemplified by the syllogism. The syllogism is a set of propositions in which the conclusion follows necessarily from the premises. For example:

All men are mortal.
Kim is a man.
Therefore Kim is mortal.

All birds have feathers.
Pterodactyls do not have feathers.
Therefore pterodactyls are not birds.

The development of formal logic was a major intellectual achievement and an important advance. It served humanity pretty well for 2,000 years. However, it was based on abstracting "things" from the processes of which they were part; it required that the unceasing flow of life be conceptualised as a series of photographic stills. The moment motion and change are fed into the equation and we remember that things don't just "exist" but come into being and pass out of being the laws of identity and non-contradiction are breached. Engels put it this way:

> True, so long as we consider things as at rest and lifeless, each one by itself, alongside and after each other, we do not run up against any contradictions in them... Inside the limits of this sphere of observation we can get along on the basis of the usual...mode of thought. But the position is quite different as soon as we consider things in their motion, their change, their life, their reciprocal influence in one another. Then we immediately become involved in contradictions. Motion itself is a contradiction; even simple mechanical change of position can only come about through a body being at one and the same moment of time both in one place and in another place, being in one and the same and also not in it...
>
> If simple mechanical change of position contains a contradiction this is even more true of the higher firms of motion of matter, and especially of organic life and development... Life consists precisely and primarily in this – that a being is at each moment itself and yet something else. (F Engels, *Anti-Dühring*, Moscow, 1969, pp144-145)

If anything (a grain of sand, a mountain, a tree, a fish, a human, a society) gives the appearance of stability and permanence it is because it constitutes a particular moment in a longer process of change. That moment constitutes a particular balance between forces within it working for and against change – a unity of opposites; much as the earth's, or any planet's, orbit around the sun represents a balance between the force of gravity pulling it into the sun and the momentum which would send it flying off into space. Trotsky approaches the same point from a different angle:

> The Aristotelian logic of the simple syllogism starts from the proposition that "A" is equal to "A"... But in reality "A" is not equal to "A". This is easy to prove if we observe these letters under a lens. But one can object, the question is not of the size or the form of the letters since they are only symbols for equal quantities, for instance a pound of sugar. The objection is beside the point; in reality a pound of sugar is never equal to a pound of sugar...all bodies change, uninterruptedly in size, weight, colour, etc... Thus the axiom A is equal to A signifies that a thing is equal to itself if it does not change, that is, if it does not exist. (L Trotsky, *In Defence of Marxism*, London 1966, pp64-65)

Dialectics then is a logic, a science of the forms of thought, designed to go beyond the limitations of formal logic. It is the logic of change, development and evolution, and therefore also of revolution. Dialectics develops and deploys a series of "laws" or "principles" which express the inner logic of change and are therefore extremely useful for the analysis of change of all kinds, especially social change. Among these principles are: the standpoint of totality, the standpoint of the concrete, the unity of opposites, the transformation of quantity into quality, the negation of the negation. I will say a little about each.

The standpoint of totality

No phenomenon or incident, especially no political phenomenon, can be properly understood or analysed in isolation. It is always necessary to see it in its context and its interrelations, and not only with the events and circumstances immediately adjacent to it, but in relation to the overall picture of world capitalism, the international class struggle, their historical development and their present state. No war, strike, demonstration, campaign, issue, etc can be treated in abstraction from the life of the society as a whole.

Contemporary politics provides many examples of this principle. In Ireland, as I write, there is something of a mass revolt over the issue of Household Charges – a 100-euro flat tax on all homeowners. Half the country is refusing to pay. The tax is unfair in itself because people in poverty will pay the same as millionaires, but virtually everybody involved knows there is more than this at stake. Resistance to the Household Charge has become a focus for, and symbol of, general anger and resistance to the massive cuts and severe austerity measures being imposed by the Irish government to pay for enormous bail-out given to the Irish banks. This in turn is not an isolated national issue but part of the overall crisis of capitalism that burst into the open in the US in 2008.

Similarly the conflict in Palestine cannot be grasped as a merely local dispute between Palestinians and Israelis or Arabs and Jews. Why is Israel able to get away with ongoing atrocities against the Palestinians and repeated violations of international law, such as violently intercepting ships on the high seas, without any sanctions or punishment by the so-called "international community"? Because it has the backing of the US and its allies. Why do they back Israel? Because Israel serves as a loyal watchdog for the interests of Western imperialism in the Middle East, which is of vital importance because it contains such a high proportion of the world's oil supplies. People who fail to grasp this overall context often imagine that the conflict can be resolved by persuading Palestinians and Israelis to compromise and get along with one another but this is an illusion based on a complete misunderstanding of the situation. Neither this conflict nor any of the other conflicts in the Middle East can be assessed in isolation from the total struggle between imperialism and the international working class and the oppressed.

The standpoint of totality, it is worth noting, is simultaneously a philosophical principle of dialectics and a political principle of the workers' movement. This is not coincidence for the working class is precisely the universal class, whose liberation will liberate humanity as a whole and whose liberation requires the total transformation of society. Moreover the criterion by which every issue is assessed is the interests of the working class as a whole.

The standpoint of the concrete

"Truth is concrete," Lenin (following Hegel) used to say. At first sight this may seem at odds with the principle of totality. In reality it complements it. Yes every individual event must be related to the whole but it does not thereby lose its specificity. The relation of the part to the whole is a specific relation of a specific part to a specific whole and they mutually condition one another. The example of war is again very useful here. War is, in general, caused by class society and modern war is caused by capitalism. But not all wars, not even all capitalist wars, are the same or equally reactionary. The American War of Independence, the American Civil War (against the South) and the American war in Vietnam were all capitalist wars, but the first two were progressive and third thoroughly reactionary. The war of Iraq against Iran (1980-88) was – because of its relationship to US imperialism – reactionary. The war by the same Iraqi regime against the US in 1990-91 and again in 2003 was progressive, despite the despotic and reactionary nature of the Iraq regime. The Spanish Civil War (on the part of the Republic) was progressive and was seen as such by the working class internationally; the Korean War, by virtue of each side's relationship to US and Russian imperialism respectively, was reactionary on both sides. The reader may disagree with these particular assessments but the point is in each case it is necessary to make a concrete analysis of the concrete situation.

The transformation of quantity into quality

This refers to the relationship between continuity and change discussed earlier. How does one thing become something else? How does water become steam, an infant become a child, and then an adult, an economic boom turn into a slump, one social system, feudalism, turn into another, capitalism? In each case a process occurs in which there is a gradual accumulation of quantitative changes within the given totality up to a point where there is a sudden or relatively sudden transformation in the nature of the totality as a whole. The molecules in a litre of water are progressively excited through the application of heat, the temperature of water rises but it remains water, then at around 100°C, a turning point is reached and suddenly the water starts to boil, ie transform into steam.

The capitalist economic boom is firing on all cylinders – profits rise, investment rises, production rises, employment and wages increase, then within the framework of the boom, imperceptibly at first, countertendencies start to appear – investment in fixed capital starts to increase in proportion to investment in labour, lowering the overall rate of profit; production rises to a point where it exceeds what the market can bear; wage increases start to eat into profits. All of a sudden, sometimes literally overnight, the market crashes and the boom turns into a slump in which investment falls, production falls and employment and wages fall.

The importance of this principle for politics should be obvious. I will discuss the most important instance, the transformation of the social system, in the next section on historical materialism, but the relevance of quantitative and qualitative change for the relationship between the struggle for reform and the struggle for revolution is clear. There is an excellent dialectical discussion of this question in Rosa Luxemburg's famous booklet *Reform or Revolution*:

> At first view the title of this work may be found surprising. Can the Social-Democracy [the Marxists – JM] be against reforms? Can we counterpose the social revolution, the transformation of the existing order, our final goal, to social reforms? Certainly not. The daily struggle for reforms, for the amelioration of the condition of the workers within the framework of the existing social order, and for democratic institutions, offers to the social democracy the only means of engaging in the proletarian class war and working in the direction of the final goal – the conquest of political power and the suppression of wage labour. Between social reforms and revolution there exists for the social democracy an indissoluble tie. The struggle for reforms is its means; the social revolution, its aim. (R Luxemburg, *Reform or Revolution*, London, 1989, p21)

And:

> Every legal constitution is the *product* of a revolution...in each historic period work for reforms is carried on only in

> the framework of the social form created by the last revolution. Here is the kernel of the problem.
>
> It is contrary to history to represent work for reforms as a long drawn out revolution and revolution as a condensed series of reforms. A social transformation and a legislative reform do not differ according to their duration but according to their content. The secret of historic change through the utilisation of political power resides precisely in the transformation of simple quantitative modification into a new quality, or to speak more concretely, in the passage of an historic period from one given form of society to another. (as above, pp74-75)

Then there is that central question of revolutionary strategy: determination of the moment when molecular changes in the consciousness and confidence of the masses permits the transition from the methods of propaganda and agitation to the direct organisation of revolutionary insurrection. Or conversely, the problem of determining when the revolutionary tide has ebbed and the wave of reaction or direct counter-revolution has set in. As Trotsky says, "To determine at the right moment the critical point where quantity changes into quality is one of the most important and difficult tasks in all the spheres of knowledge including sociology" (L Trotsky, *In Defence of Marxism*, as above, p65).

The defeat of the 1905 Revolution in Russia was followed by a period of severe reaction (1907-10) in which the Bolsheviks more or less collapsed. Lenin, argues Trotsky, was "extremely late retreating" and "this aggravated the decline" (*Trotsky's Notebooks, 1933-35: Writings on Lenin, Dialectics and Evolutionism*, New York, 1986, p80). But in the revolution of 1917 Lenin was masterly in his ability to judge crucial turning points, especially the moment when insurrection became both possible and necessary.

The unity of opposites

The transformation of quantitative into qualitative change just described presupposes that the object or given totality which changes is a unity of opposites – a (temporary) balance of conflicting forces. This applies to everything from a single atom (which consists of a dense central nucleus surrounded by a cloud of negatively charged electrons with the nucleus itself containing a mix of positively charged protons and electrically neutral neutrons*) to the US New World Order (a "balance" between US power and anti-imperialist resistance and many other conflicting forces). Even an apparently lifeless object like a wooden chair is simply a relatively stable moment between the forces bringing it into being and its eventual disintegration, between a living tree and a pile of dust.

Lenin in his brief 1915 notes "On the Question of Dialectics" puts, in my opinion rightly, particular emphasis on this aspect of dialectics:

> The splitting of a single whole and the cognition of its contradictory parts is the *essence* (one of the "essentials", one of the principal, if not the principal, characteristics or features) of dialectics...
>
> [The unity of opposites] is the recognition (discovery) of the contradictory, mutually exclusive, opposite tendencies in all phenomena and processes of nature (including mind and society). The condition of knowledge of all processes of the world in their "self-movement", is the knowledge of them as development, in their real life, is knowledge of them as a unity of

* This is the classical image of an atom. Quantum physics gives a deeper, more complex model of the atom which is beyond the range of this book.

> opposites. Development is the "struggle" of opposites. (V I Lenin, *Collected Works*, Vol 38, Moscow, 1963, p359)

Lenin also insists that in the concept of the unity of opposites the element of "balance" or stability is secondary and the element of conflict leading to "leaps", to the "break in continuity", to "transformation into the opposite", to the destruction of the old and the emergence of the new, is fundamental.

> The unity (coincidence, identity, equal action) of opposites is conditional, temporary, transitional, relative. The struggle of mutually exclusive opposites is absolute, just as development and motion are absolute (as above, p359).

Thus Mount Everest is a unity of opposites – the collision of tectonic plates that thrust it upwards and the forces of erosion that wear it down – but where this really matters is in the analysis of concrete political situations, regimes and phases in the class struggle.

The negation of the negation

This is another term from Hegel used on occasion by Marx and Engels to capture the dialectical process. It expresses the fact that when a given state changes on the basis of its internal contradictions the force for change, the antithesis or negation, is itself changed (negated) and the outcome both retains some elements from the past and constitutes a new state (or synthesis) which is more than the sum of its previous parts.

This may sound complicated but the much-used example to illustrate it, the transition from capitalism to socialism, does, I hope, make it clear.

Capitalism develops into socialism, not gradually but through a struggle between opposed forces, the bourgeoisie and the proletariat. The proletariat is the antithesis or negation of capitalism and the bourgeoisie, but it does not simply destroy capitalism or disband it; it necessarily has to retain and take over a large part of the scientific, industrial and cultural heritage from the past. At the same time the proletariat, in overthrowing capitalism, becomes the new ruling class and begins the process of establishing a classless socialist society in which the proletariat ceases to be a distinct separate class, ie is negated.

Engels also uses such examples as the life cycle of barley from grain to flower to refertilisation and of butterflies from egg to caterpillar to chrysalis, to imago and more eggs, each illustrating the principle of change through successive negations (F Engels, *Anti-Dühring*, as above, pp162-163).

It should be said that some Marxists have rejected the negation of the negation because of the deterministic use made of it by Stalinism, in which the replacement of feudalism by capitalism and capitalism by socialism (the negation of the negation) was depicted as a natural law and therefore inevitable. Such determinism was in turn used to bolster the authority of the party leadership by presenting it as the embodiment of predetermined historical destiny. But if we throw out concepts on the grounds of their distortion by Stalinism we will end up throwing out Marxism in its entirety. In fact there is no necessity for the negation of the negation to be interpreted or used in this deterministic fashion. If I demonstrate that for a baby to reach old age it must pass through certain stages of development – infancy, childhood, adolescence, adulthood, middle age – I do not thereby prove or even claim that, in any particular case, this will inevitably happen (as opposed to the process being interrupted by premature death), or that in every case the process will be exactly the same, or that it is not necessary actively to intervene in and assist the process.

This argument, by the way, applies to deterministic interpretations of dialectics as a whole. Dialectics grasps and reflects the logic of natural and social change, but it does not, in itself, prove (and should not claim to prove) that any specific change will inevitably occur.

A substantial debate has existed in the history of Marxism as to whether the dialectic applies to nature, as Engels maintained, or should be restricted to the field of human history. The controversy began with a footnote criticising Engels in Hungarian Marxist Georg Lukács's *History and Class Consciousness* in 1923:

> It is of the first importance to realise that the method is limited here to the realms of history and society. The misunderstandings that arise from Engels' account of dialectics can in the main be put down to the fact that Engels – following Hegel's mistaken lead – extended the method to apply also to nature. However, the crucial determinants of dialectics – the interaction of subject and object, the unity of theory and practice, the historical changes in the reality underlying the categories as the root cause of changes in thought, etc – are absent from our knowledge of nature. (G Lukács, *History and Class Consciousness*, London, 1971, p24n)

This argument was then taken up by a wide variety of Marxist philosophers (and commentators on Marx) including Karl Korsch, Herbert Marcuse, Louis Althusser, Jean-Paul Sartre, Lucio Colletti, Alfred Schmidt and Terrell Carver, whereas the dialectics of nature were defended by Lenin, Trotsky, Luxemburg, Gramsci and scientists such as J B S Haldane (see Haldane's Preface to F Engels, *Dialectics of Nature*, London, 1941) and R C Lewontin (see R C Lewontin and R Levins, *The Dialectical Biologist*, Harvard, 1985).

As to where Marx himself stood, this is part of the debate. Opponents of the dialectics of nature generally attribute the idea to Engels who developed it in *Anti-Dühring* and *The Dialectics of Nature*, while claiming that it does not appear in Marx. Defenders of the dialectics of nature retort that Marx persuaded Engels to write *Anti-Dühring* and is known to have read the manuscript before publication, and that it is entirely improbable that Marx and Engels, on the basis of over 30 years of the closest intellectual collaboration, would have been unaware of a major philosophical disagreement, especially as they were both keenly interested in the natural sciences. (I should say that, personally, I find this retort very convincing.) Moreover in *Capital*, Vol 1, Marx, in dealing with "the sum of value that the individual possessor of money or commodities must command, in order to metamorphose himself into a capitalist", explicitly states, "Here, as in natural science, is shown the correctness of the law discovered by Hegel (in his 'Logic'), that merely quantitative differences beyond a certain point pass into qualitative changes" (K Marx, *Capital*, Vol 1, London, 1974, p292*).

As to the issue itself, Engels's critics variously maintain: (a) that the dialectics of nature idea was taken over uncritically from Hegel; (b) that it reflects the influence of 19th century positivism's uncritical enthusiasm for science; (c) that Marxism should be seen as a critique of capitalism, not an all-encompassing worldview; (d) that there is no such thing as contradictions in nature; (e) that, as Lukács said, "the interaction between subject and object" is a crucial determinant of dialectics but is absent from nature.

It is not possible to offer a full account of this debate

---

* I am indebted to Joseph Choonara for this point.

here* but my own view is as follows:

Marx and Engels openly proclaimed their debt to Hegel in the matter of dialectics, but Engels was a strong critic of mechanical materialism and 19th century positivism.

Human beings emerge out of nature and remain part of it and therefore Gramsci's objection to Lukács that "If his assertion proposes a dualism between nature and man he is wrong" (A Gramsci, *Selections from the Prison Notebooks*, London, 1982, p448) is valid.

Marxism is not only a critique of capitalism but, as Gramsci says, "contains in itself all the fundamental elements needed to construct a total and integral conception of the world, a total philosophy and theory of natural science" (A Gramsci, as above, p462).

There *are* contradictions in nature, as seen in examples I have given above, between forces bringing a certain natural state or object into being and forces bringing about its ceasing to be.

Dialectics is fundamentally the logic of change and development and therefore applies to science and nature since change and development are all-pervasive in nature. The absence of the subjective factor does not rule out the application of dialectics to nature. This doesn't mean natural history and human history are the same – the role of consciousness (the subjective factor) makes a difference as both Engels and Trotsky explicitly recognise (see F Engels, *Ludwig Feuerbach and the End of Classical German Philosophy*, Peking, 1976, p40 and *Trotsky's Notebooks*, as above, p102).

---

* A good historical overview is to be found in H Sheehan, *Marxism and the Philosophy of Science*, New Jersey, 1993. For a strong defence of Engels see *The Revolutionary Ideas of Frederick Engels*, *International Socialism* 65 (winter 1994), especially P McGarr, "Engels and Natural Science".

For all these reasons I believe dialectics *is* applicable to nature and is a very useful guide to scientific investigation. However, it needs to be understood that the "laws of the dialectic" identified by Hegel and Engels ("the transformation of quantity into quality", "the unity (or interpenetration) of opposites" and "the negation of the negation" (See F Engels, *The Dialectics of Nature,* as above, p26) are not "laws of nature" in the same sense as the law of gravity or the laws of motion. They do not yield more or less mathematically precise and accurate predictions; rather they are guidelines or laws of logic which apply in, and assist the development of, natural science because they reflect and express, better than formal logic, the actual processes of change, development and evolution in nature.

I want to conclude this section by stressing the importance of dialectics for revolutionary practice. Clearly a theory which identifies the logic of change is going to be useful to those who want to change the world. Where Marx is concerned it is evident that dialectics underpins and pervades his entire theoretical output from the early *Economic and Philosophic Manuscripts* to the late *Critique of the Gotha Programme* and particularly his masterwork, *Capital.* The same can be said for all the pre-eminent Marxist theoreticians – Engels, Lenin, Trotsky, Luxemburg and Gramsci.

The history of the Marxist movement shows that there have been a number of occasions when the conscious application of dialectics has played a major role in the solution of key political problems. Perhaps the most important and dramatic instance is Lenin's response to the First World War. The outbreak of the war in August 1914 did not come as a surprise to Lenin – everyone following international politics had known for sometime that a European war was likely – but the reaction of the international socialist movement as represented by the Second International most certainly did.

Prior to 1914 the International had clearly and consistently opposed the prospect of war but when it actually broke out the majority of the leaders of European socialism, and above all of the German SPD (the leading party of International), abandoned their anti-war stance and supported their own imperialist governments. In the German parliament only one, Karl Liebknecht, out of the SPD's 111 deputies voted against war credits for the government. This came as a profound shock to Lenin – it turned his world upside down. He responded, characteristically, by reaffirming his opposition to the war in the strongest terms possible, but also by a root and branch reassessment of the Marxism of the Second International, and to make that reassessment he returned to Hegel and the study of the dialectic.

The results of this study, marginal notes on Hegel's *Logic* and responses to other texts, are to be found in Volume 38 of Lenin's *Collected Works*. They reveal a real development, a qualitative leap in Lenin's Marxism, in which he takes issue with the rather mechanical and deterministic interpretation spread by the leaders of the Second International such as Karl Kautsky in Germany and George Plekhanov in Russia. "It is impossible", proclaims Lenin, "completely to understand Marx's *Capital*, and especially its first chapter, without having thoroughly studied and understood the whole of Hegel's *Logic*. Consequently, half a century later none of the Marxists understood Marx!" (V I Lenin, *Collected Works*, Vol 38, as above, p180) And in opposition to Plekhanov and Kautsky's mechanical view of thought and ideas as a simple reflection of material reality (previously shared by Lenin himself), he argues, "The *reflection* of nature in man's thought must be understood not 'lifelessly', not 'abstractly', *not devoid of movement, not without contradictions*, but in the eternal *process* of movement, the arising of contradictions and their solution" (as above, p195).

The political consequences of this philosophical mini-revolution were immediately seen in some of Lenin's greatest works. In *Imperialism: The Highest Stage of Capitalism* (published in 1916), he showed how quantitative changes in capitalism, the concentration of production and the growth of monopolies, led to a qualitatively new stage in capitalism – imperialism – and how that new stage, far from overcoming the system's internal contradictions, reproduced them on a new level, thus laying the basis for the imperialist world war. In other writings on imperialism he showed how this new stage of development had transformed the upper layers of the socialist movement into accomplices of the system but it had simultaneously generated new forces of opposition and revolution in the shape of anti-imperialist revolt by oppressed nations (such as Ireland and China). Then in 1917 in *The State and Revolution* and the *April Theses* Lenin both restored the authentic Marxist theory of the state – that the working class would need to smash the existing capitalist state apparatus rather than simply taking it over (which had been the teaching of the Second International) – and deepened it by showing that the soviets (or workers' councils) thrown up in course of the Russian Revolution were the embryo of the new workers' state apparatus.

In these post-1914 writings Lenin's conscious application of dialectical thinking is very much in evidence. The same is true in his debates with the inexperienced ultra-left trends that emerged in the early years of the Communist International (the new network of revolutionary organisations initiated by Lenin after the Second International collapsed). The issues contested at that time are still relevant for the movement now and they serve as good examples of the usefulness of dialectics for today's activists. One such issue was participation in parliamentary elections. Revolutionary Marxists do not believe in a parliamentary road to socialism; nevertheless they should participate in parliamentary elections – a contradiction, surely. Yes, but one that has to be worked through, not avoided by sitting on the sidelines. Revolutionaries, Lenin argued, must take part in elections as part of the struggle for the consciousness of the masses, who *do* still believe in parliament in order to develop the struggle *against* parliament from inside parliament. Parliamentary elections are an arena of ideological and political struggle which must not simply be abandoned to the bourgeois and reformist parties (for Lenin's arguments on this see *Left-Wing Communism: An Infantile Disorder*).

Another was the tactic of the united front. The starting point of the Communist International, formed in 1919, was the necessity of a political and organisational break with the reformist parties of the Second International – the formation of independent revolutionary parties. But then in 1921, after the immediate post-war revolutionary wave had receded and capitalism had temporarily stabilised itself, Lenin and Trotsky argued that it was necessary to form a united front with these same social democrats against the attacks of capital. To some of the ultra-lefts this seemed a betrayal. Lenin and Trotsky argued that it did not mean abandoning the struggle against reformism (or the independence of the revolutionary party) but pursuing that struggle in a new way – putting pressure on the reformist leaders and exposing their inability to fight while simultaneously maximising the fighting strength of the working class (see for example, L Trotsky, *The First Five Years of the Communist International*, Vol 2, London, 1973, pp91-96).

The united front was and remains an excellent example of dialectics in action, but on this matter one further – dialectical – point needs to be made. History, as we have seen, always involves both continuity and change and this applies here. The united front cannot today take the same form as it did in the 1920s (or as Trotsky advocated in the

1930s against fascism). This is because what they envisaged was essentially a formal alliance between a mass Communist Party and a mass Social Democratic Party. Today, in most parts of the world, neither of these forces exists in the way they once did. In particular the Social Democratic Parties, having embraced neoliberalism, are often the enemy against whom the united front would need to be organised. However, this does not mean giving up the united front tactic, for the contradiction it was designed to address – the need of the working class for ideological and political clarity on the one hand, and for maximum unity in the immediate struggle on the other – is still very much with us. What it means therefore is finding new forms for the united front, such as in the anti-war movement and the anti-cuts campaigns or Unite Against Fascism.

It would be silly and futile to demand of all revolutionary activists that they acquaint themselves with Hegel and master the dialectic of nature, just as it would be to expect that all revolutionary workers, especially in a mass movement and a mass party, read *Capital* and *The German Ideology*. Nevertheless, because it captures the inner logic of change the materialist dialectic of Marx and Engels is an exceptionally useful tool for the analysis and practical solution of the innumerable problems thrown up by the class struggle, which is itself a dialectical process par excellence.

6. Historical materialism

Marx's theory of history, or historical materialism as it is known, is the materialist dialectic applied to the sphere of human history. It is also, in a sense, the core theory of Marxism as a whole. Engels, when summarising Marx's theoretical achievements in his speech at his graveside in 1883, gave pride of place to historical materialism: "Just as Darwin discovered the law of development of organic nature, so Marx discovered the law of development of human history" (K Marx and F Engels, *Selected Works*, Vol 2, as above, p167). Marx himself called it "the guiding principle of my studies" (D McLellan, ed, as above, p389). Indeed historical materialism is sometimes used as a synonym for Marxist theory in its totality. It is what structures a Marxist view of the overall development of human history and where contemporary society, including our own struggles within that society, fit into the larger picture. It is the starting point (here I emphasise starting point) that Marxists use every day for the analysis of current events and ideological arguments.

Base and superstructure

The starting point of historical materialism is extremely simple and clearly set out by Marx and Engels in *The German Ideology*:

> The premises from which we begin are not arbitrary ones, not dogmas, but real premises from which abstraction can only be made in the imagination. They are the real individuals, their activity and the material conditions under which they live...

> The first premise of all human history is, of course, the existence of living human individuals. Thus the first fact to be established is the physical organisation of these individuals and their consequent relation to the rest of nature. (D McLellan, ed, as above, p161)

The physical organisation of humans determines that in order to live, even for days or weeks, they require water, food, shelter, perhaps clothing, etc. Moreover, as we have seen, human beings distinguished themselves from animals by actively producing these means of subsistence (through social labour and cultural tool-making). From this it follows that the foundation for the analysis of all human historical development and every human society is production and how it is organised.

In analysing human production Marx then made a very important (we shall see its full importance a bit later) conceptual distinction between "forces of production" and "relations of production". The forces of production are those things which make up a society's general capacity to produce goods – its natural resources, labour and technology (including the knowledge to make and use that technology). The relations of production are the social relations that people enter into in order to engage in production. The development of the wheel, iron tools, the windmill, the steam engine, the computer and contemporary China's vast supply of labour are all examples of the advance of the productive forces. An aboriginal hunting party, a slave working on the estate of a Roman patrician, a medieval serf ploughing his lord's land, a tenant farmer paying rent to his landlord, Henry Ford employing thousands of workers in his motor company and Wal-Mart employing over 2 million people worldwide, are all examples of relations of production.

Clearly forces and relations of production are not separate entities – you can't have "forces" without "relations" or "relations" without "forces" – but two aspects of a single process which continually interact and influence each other. However, Marx identified one of the aspects, the forces of production, as more fundamental and ultimately more dynamic and decisive than the other. At bottom it is the level of development of the forces of production which conditions or shapes the relations of production. However, and this is important, this "conditioning" is not a mechanical or absolute determinism. A society in which the productive forces permit only hunting and gathering, as was the case for most of human history, produces the social relations of the small nomadic hunting clans. The development of agriculture and with it settled communities (villages and towns) and the ability to create and store a surplus of produce over and above what is needed for immediate survival give rise to the differentiation between rich and poor, to class divisions and to such production relations as slavery and later, serfdom. Manufacturing and modern industrial production bring with them the production relation of wage labour. Here it is important to note that these capitalist relations of production exercise a major influence on the development of the productive forces, both driving them forward because of the dynamic of competitive capital accumulation in booms and fettering or throwing them back in crises, but this does not change the ultimate primacy of the productive forces in this dialectical relationship.

This combination of forces and relations of production results in the formation of a series of modes of production, definite socio-economic systems which dominate whole epochs of human history. Broadly speaking we can identify the following modes of production: hunting and gathering or primitive communism; ancient (slave) society; the Asiatic mode of production (traditional India,

China, etc); feudalism; capitalism.*

It is not possible to give exact dates for these modes of production particularly as they last for different lengths of time in different parts of the world – for example primitive communism ceased to be the dominant mode of production with the development of agriculture about 12,000 to 8,000 years ago, but continued to exist in some places, such as the Kalahari Desert, well into the 20th century, and serfdom died out in England in the 14th century but survived in Russia until 1861. However, it is useful to give a very rough periodisation, especially for the newcomer to these concepts. Thus ancient society, or the slave mode of production, refers to the societies of Ancient Egypt, Greece, Rome and elsewhere and comes to an end with the collapse of the Roman Empire in the 5th century AD. It is succeeded, in Europe, by feudalism, which lasts through the Middle Ages and starts to be superseded by capitalism in the 16th century. Capitalism achieves its initial breakthroughs in Holland and England and becomes the dominant system in the world with the French Revolution of 1789-94 and the industrial revolution in Britain. The Asiatic mode of production survives until it is overwhelmed by European capitalist imperialism.

Many people believe that in the 20th century a whole range of countries – the Soviet Union, Eastern Europe, China, North Korea, Vietnam, Cuba, etc – passed beyond capitalism and became socialist. In the author's opinion this was and is an illusion and, with the exception of the early years of the

---

* This list is not exhaustive. There may have been other modes of production and there is debate among Marxist historians about the concept of the Asiatic mode of production (is it distinct or a version of feudalism?) and about the mode of production in Aztec and Inca societies, for example, but these questions need not detain us here.

Russian Revolution, these countries were state capitalist, ie they were versions of the capitalist mode of production.

In forming the mode of production, the forces and relations of production also constitute the economic base of society on which, Marx says, "rises a legal and political superstructure and to which correspond definite forms of social consciousness. The mode of production of material life conditions the social, political and intellectual life process in general" (D McLellan, ed, as above, p389). This brings us back to the point about social being determining consciousness already discussed in the section on materialism. For Marx politics, philosophy, religion, art, etc are all part of the superstructure and their development depends on and is conditioned by the development of the base. Any major change in social consciousness – for example the secularisation process in Europe or the rise of nationalism – has its roots in changes in the forces and relations of production. The relationship here is by no means simple or mechanical. For one thing, ideas have a tendency to cling on and survive after their immediate material basis has disappeared. "The tradition of all the dead generations weighs like a nightmare on the brain of the living," writes Marx in *The Eighteenth Brumaire of Louis Bonaparte* (D McLellan, ed, as above, p300), explaining why Martin Luther "donned the mask of the Apostle Paul" and the French Revolution of 1789 draped itself as the Roman Republic. For another, the relationship between material conditions and the world of ideas can be an inverted one (as in a "camera obscura", as Marx puts it). Thus the English romantic poets and artists (Wordsworth, Coleridge, Constable, Turner, etc) turned to nature themes at just the moment that, and *because*, Britain was going through its industrial revolution and massive urbanisation was taking place. Nevertheless, the relationship is real and all historical materialist analysis of political and intellectual life sets out from this premise.

The most important element in the superstructure is the state apparatus and its legal system. By this is meant a cluster of interlinked institutions including the armed forces, the security services, the government, ministries, parliament, the police, the judiciary, the prisons, etc. Between them these institutions lay claim to ultimate authority in society and the sole right to exercise serious physical force. Crucially, in modern society, the state also lays claim to political and social neutrality. It is presented and presents itself as standing outside and above the conflicts between different interest groups and shades of opinion, like an unbiased referee.

Marx rejects this as self-serving myth. For Marx the state is never neutral but always directly or indirectly the state of the economically dominant class and its primary function is the preservation of the existing social and economic order. "The executive of the modern state", says Marx in the *Communist Manifesto*, "is nothing but a committee for managing the common affairs of the whole bourgeoisie" (D McLellan, ed, as above, p223). Likewise the law is not a set of eternal or abstract principles but a codification of the property relations, relations of production and behaviour patterns required by a particular mode of production.

Sometimes – Nazi Germany is an example – the state, in terms of its personnel and policies, can be detached from the direct control of the economically dominant class. An earlier example, that of Napoleon III (nephew of Napoleon I), Emperor of France 1852-70, was analysed by Marx in *The Eighteenth Brumaire of Louis Napoleon*, hence the phenomenon became known as "Bonapartism". But even in these exceptional cases the state rests fundamentally on an economic base which it is required to maintain and defend.

As Marx showed in practice in *The Eighteenth Brumaire*, and as Engels was at pains to explain in a series of letters written towards the end of his life, historical materialism does not maintain or imply a mechanical or rigid relationship between base and superstructure. It is not, as has often been alleged, a theory of economic determinism. Rather there is a complex and dialectical interaction between base and superstructure in which certain elements develop a degree of autonomy and exercise a definite influence in the course of history. Engels writes:

> The economic situation is the basis, but the various elements of the superstructure – political forms of the class struggle and its results...juridical forms... The reflexes of all these actual struggles, in the brains of the participants, political, juristic, philosophical theories, and religious views also exercise their influence on the cause of the historical struggles and in many cases preponderate in determining their form. (K Marx and F Engels, *Selected Works*, Vol 2, as above, p488)

Nevertheless the base, human productive activity, remains primary and all historical analysis, all theory, must proceed from the base to the superstructure, not the other way round. This is a core proposition of Marxism, because as Engels said, "mankind must first of all eat, drink, have shelter and clothing before it can pursue politics, science, art, religion, etc" (as above, p167).

Forces and relations of production

Historical materialism's most important task is to explain the dynamic of history and in particular how one mode of production changes (and therefore can be changed) into another. For Marx the precondition for such a change is the development of a contradiction between the forces of production and the relations of production. As we have seen, the productive forces condition the relations of production and, therefore, at first these relations assist or allow the further development of the productive forces. But over time the productive forces continue to grow – historical materialism assumes a general tendency towards such growth simply because human beings will tend to find more effective ways of producing goods – until they reach the point where their further development requires the establishment of new relations:

> At a certain stage of development the material productive forces of society came into conflict with the existing relations of production or – this merely expresses the same thing in legal terms – with the property relations within the framework of which they have operated hitherto. From forms of development of the productive forces these relations turn into their fetters. Then begins an era of social revolution. (D McLellan, ed, as above, p389)

Note that the contradiction between the forces and relations of production is not resolved smoothly or automatically but through revolution. To understand how and why this is the case we have to put flesh on the abstractions of forces and relations of production. As we have seen in the section on class struggle, the relations of production of a society form the basis of its class structure. Indeed from the moment humankind moved beyond primitive communism, the fundamental relations of production, ie those relating to ownership and control of the means and process of production, *are* class relations – between slave owners and slaves, lords and serfs, capitalists and workers. Thus in any mode of production there is a dominant or ruling class which has a vested interest in the preservation of the existing society. Moreover this class has at its disposal the power of the state and ideology. As Marx says, "The ideas of the ruling class are in every epoch the ruling ideas, ie the class which is the ruling material force of society is at the same time its ruling intellectual force" (D McLellan, ed, as above, p176).

Likewise the forces of production do not consist only of technology but also of the human beings whose labour and knowledge work that technology – they form a social class or classes. The contradiction between the developing forces of production and the old or existing relations of production is therefore at the same time a class struggle. The class struggle, the struggle between the exploiters and the exploited, is, of course, continuous. But it is the development of the conflict between the forces and relations of production to the point where it throws society into crisis that creates the possibility of defeat for the ruling class and victory for the oppressed class.

Equally the change from one mode of production to another is put on the historical agenda by the conflict between the forces and relations of production coming to a head, but its actual achievement requires the revolutionary overthrow of the old ruling class by a new rising class linked to the developing forces of production. Moreover, experience has shown that the outcome of this revolutionary process is by no means guaranteed in advance. It depends partly on objective factors such as the depth of the crisis in society and the relative size and economic strength of the opposed classes, but also on subjective factors such as the level of consciousness, organisation and, crucially, political leadership of the revolutionary class.

In this brief account of historical materialism I have flagged up several issues – the way in which Marxism is not a philosophy of economic determinism, the role of ideology and the role of political leadership – which will be taken up and explored further in subsequent chapters.

7. The contradictions of capitalism

One of the fundamental differences between Marxist socialism and earlier forms of socialism, such as that of Fourier, Saint-Simon and Owen, the so-called "utopians", was that for Marx socialism was not a "good idea" or recipe for a perfect society dreamt up by himself or any other thinker, but a new mode of production that would emerge out of, and on the basis of, the contradictions in capitalism:

> The theoretical conclusions of the Communists are in no way based on ideas or principles that have been invented, or discovered, by this or that would-be universal reformer.
>
> They merely express, in general terms, actual relations springing from an existing class struggle, from a historical movement going on under our very eyes. (*The Communist Manifesto*, in D McLellan, ed, as above, p231)

At the most general level the fundamental contradiction in capitalism identified by Marx is that between the forces and the relations of production which we have just discussed and which, as we have seen, is at the same time a class struggle between the bourgeoisie (resting on, and with a vested interest in, the old capitalist production relations) and the proletariat (part of and linked to the developing productive forces). This contradiction is also much explored by Engels in *Anti-Dühring* (especially Part III, chapter 2). But Marx went further than this. He also identified certain specific contradictions, themselves deriving from the fundamental contradiction, which would plunge capitalism into recurring crises and thus intensify the class struggle.

The most important of these were the tendency to overproduction and the tendency of the rate of profit to decline.

Overproduction means producing more goods than can be sold (not more than are needed by people). The tendency to overproduction derives from the capitalists' drive, especially in a boom, to produce more and more combined with the fact that they pay workers less than the value of the goods they produce so that the system contains a built-in possibility of insufficient effective demand for the goods and services on the market. The declining rate of profit refers to the decline in profit as a ratio of the capitalists' total outlay on raw materials, machinery and labour. This derives from the fact that each capitalist tends to increase their expenditure on what Marx calls constant capital (raw materials, machinery, etc) more than their expenditure on labour because by so doing that capitalist initially increases their share of the total surplus value (profit), but because surplus value comes only from living labour (the actual labour performed by workers), not from dead labour (past labour congealed into machinery – ie constant capital) this has the overall effect of lowering the rate of profit in the system as a whole.

Either of these contradictions – overproduction or the declining rate of profit – can cause an economic crisis in which production falls and unemployment increases, but there are obvious ways in which each contradiction can be overcome. Overproduction can be countered by raising the purchasing power of the masses (through higher wages or government spending programmes) and the declining rate of profit can be halted by cutting wages and increasing the rate of exploitation. Unfortunately the solution to each contradiction tends to exacerbate the other one. Raising wages tends to hit profits; cutting wages increases the problem of overproduction.

Historically these contradictions have operated on different time scales. Overproduction tends to work cyclically generating the classic boom/slump "trade cycle". The declining rate of profit tends to work more slowly making, unless it is offset, slumps or recessions more severe over time.*

Another major contradiction identified by Marx was the tendency of capitalist competition to turn into its opposite – monopoly. In competition, says Marx, "one capitalist always kills many" (K Marx, *Capital*, Vol 1, as above, p714). And since victory in competition usually goes to the larger capitalist over the smaller, the ownership and control of production becomes concentrated in ever fewer hands, while the actual process of production becomes ever more socialised:

> Hand in hand with this centralisation, or this expropriation of many capitalists by few, develop, on an ever-extending scale, the cooperative form of the labour process, the conscious technical application of science, the methodical cultivation of the soil, the transformation of the instruments of labour into instruments of labour only usable in common, the economising of all means of production by their use as means of production of combined, socialised labour, the entanglement of all peoples in the net of the world market, and with this, the international character of the capitalistic regime. (as above, p714)

---

* As this is a book on Marxist philosophy not Marxist economics I have given only the very briefest account of these points, just enough to indicate their role in historical materialism as a whole. The literature on the Marxist theory of economic crisis, apart from Marx's own writings, is vast. For a very clear and accessible introductory account see J Choonara, *Unravelling Capitalism*, London, 2009. For a more advanced, detailed explanation and application see C Harman, *Explaining the Crisis*, London, 1987, and C Harman, *Zombie Capitalism: Global Crisis and the Relevance of Marx*, London, 2009.

In any given society Marx argues the limit of this centralisation would be "when the entire social capital was united in the hands of either a single capitalist or a single capitalist company" (as above, p588). And Engels pursues the logic of this contradiction further in *Anti-Dühring* saying that the process of centralisation of capital would lead ultimately to:

> partial recognition of the social character of the productive forces forced upon the capitalists themselves. Taking over of the great institutions for production and communication, first by joint-stock companies, later by trusts, then by the State. The bourgeoisie demonstrated to be a superfluous class. All its social functions are now performed by salaried employees. (F Engels, *Anti-Dühring*, Moscow, 1969, p338)

The generation of Marxists following Marx and Engels saw the rapid development of the concentration and centralisation of capital and the growth of the global economy to the point where they concluded a new stage of capitalism had been established which they called monopoly capitalism and/or imperialism. In the most influential Marxist text of the period, *Imperialism: The Highest Stage of Capitalism*, Lenin summed up imperialism as:

> capitalism at that stage of development at which the dominance of monopolies and finance capital has established itself; in which the export of capital has acquired pronounced importance; in which the division of the world among the international trusts has begun; in which the division of all territories of the globe among the biggest capitalist powers has been completed. (V I Lenin, *Imperialism: The Highest Stage of Capitalism*, Peking, 1973, p106)

For Lenin, imperialism, by means of the export of capital to regions of the world where capital was scarce and profit rates high, constituted a *partial* overcoming of the tendencies to overproduction and the falling rate of profit and, through the concentration of capital in the hands of monopolies and the state, a *partial* overcoming of the contradictions between capitals within the advanced countries, but at the same time it generated new and more deadly contradictions in that it led to a violent struggle between the Great Powers for the division and redivision of the world, ie the First World War. Moreover he argued that imperialist war intensified class contradictions to the point where it would provoke revolution ("Turn the imperialist war into a civil war!" was Lenin's slogan).

To this Lenin added the contradiction between imperialism and anti-imperialism. The imperialist takeover of the world (the colonisation of Africa, Polynesia, Asia, etc) would generate national liberation struggles which would aid the struggle of the working class to overthrow capitalism.

For these reasons Lenin characterised imperialism as an "epoch of wars and revolutions". He was proved right. The imperialist First World War led to the Russian Revolution of 1917, followed by attempted revolutions and revolutionary situations across Europe (Germany, Italy, Finland, Ireland and so on) followed later by China (1925-27) and Spain in 1936. The failure of these revolutions led to fascism and a new, even more terrible imperialist war. And imperialism produced anti-imperialist movements – almost all eventually successful in the sense of winning national independence – throughout what became known as the Third World (most importantly in India, China, Vietnam and much of Africa).

However, capitalism survived, at immense human cost, the terrible crises of the mid 20th century – the Great Depression, Nazism, Stalinism, the Second World War – and emerged into a new period of relative stability and prosperity, the post-war boom. For a period of about 25 years Western capitalism maintained more or less continuous economic growth, full employment and rising living standards. Unsurprisingly there was no shortage of claims, including from former Marxists, that capitalism had overcome its contradictions. This was largely attributed to state intervention and the economics of John Maynard Keynes. It was also said that class divisions were disappearing and the working class was becoming middle class ("bourgeoisified" as some of the sociologists put it).

But a number of Marxists, such as Tony Cliff, Mike Kidron and Chris Harman, while not denying the reality of the boom, insisted that the fundamental contradictions of the system had not disappeared. Rather they were masked for a period by what they called the permanent arms economy. Massive ongoing expenditures by the major powers on arms (especially nuclear arms) as a result of the Cold War were offsetting both the tendency to overproduction (by stimulating the economy and state employment of workers) and the declining rate of profit by draining capital out of the system (lowering the ratio between constant and variable capital) without producing goods that had to be sold on the market. But, they argued, the permanent arms economy contained its own contradictions which, once they came to the fore, would cause the underlying contradictions to reassert themselves.

Thus massive arms spending by the US and the UK created the general global conditions for sustaining the boom (by offsetting the declining rate of profit) but at the cost of retarding somewhat the growth in these specific countries. Meanwhile Germany and Japan, the defeated powers in the war (and thus restricted in their arms spending) were able to benefit from the overall expansion without having the burden of the military budgets that made it possible. This made it possible for them to grow at a much faster rate than the US and Britain – the so-called German and Japanese economic "miracles". This meant that by the end of the 1960s they were outstripping Britain and becoming serious competitors to the US, which obliged the nuclear powers to reduce their arms spending (relative to their GNP – not absolutely) which in turn meant that the declining rate of profit set in again and recessions returned to the system internationally – in 1973-74, 1979-82 and 1989-92.

As we have seen, Marx saw recessions or crises as expressions of the fundamental contradictions of capitalism, but he also argued that they functioned as a way of restoring the health of the system. This was through destroying large amounts of capital by means of bankruptcies and takeovers of the weaker firms, thus restoring the rate of profit for those that survived. But the recessions of the 1970s and 1980s were less and less able to perform this function. The concentration and centralisation of capital had created such large corporations that many of them had become "too big to fail", or rather too big to be allowed to fail by the state because the knock-on effects for the rest of the economy would be too severe.

The capitalist class internationally responded to this situation with (a) neoliberalism – in essence an attempt to increase the exploitation of workers so as to counter the falling rate of profit (witness Thatcher's and Reagan's assaults on the unions) and (b) an injection of credit to maintain the level of demand and stave off a crisis of overproduction. For a while this seemed to work, producing the expansion of 1992-2007, but in the end it just built up massive levels of unsustainable debt and made the crisis, when it came with the credit crunch of August 2007 and the collapse of Lehman Brothers and the financial crisis of 2008, all the more catastrophic. Hence the proliferation of commentators across the political spectrum who are now recognising that perhaps Marx was right after all (about the crisis-ridden nature of capitalism, not about the revolutionary role of the working class, of course).*

Finally, over the last 20 years another fundamental contradiction of the system has come to the fore: that between capitalism and nature.

As a result of Stalinism, which was fundamentally the ideology of the state capitalist industrialisation of Russia (and later, in its Maoist form, of China) Marxism came to be widely associated, particularly in the underdeveloped countries, with economic development and industrialisation rather than working class self-emancipation and human liberation.† In this process the ecological dimension of Marx's thought was largely lost sight of but, as John Bellamy Foster has powerfully demonstrated,‡ Marx was always profoundly concerned with humankind's relationship with and impact on nature. Indeed, this was a logical corollary of his thorough-going philosophical materialism and his conviction that human beings were part of nature.

Very near the start of *The German Ideology* (1845), the first systematic exposition of historical materialism, in the section on "The first premises of the materialist method", Marx and Engels write:

> The first premise of all human history is, of course, the existence of living human individuals. Thus the first fact to be established is the physical organisation of these individuals

---

* For example Nouriel Roubini, who told the *Wall Street Journal*, "Karl Marx had it right. Capitalism can self-destruct." See http://on.wsj.com/roubmarx

† See J Molyneux, *What is the Real Marxist Tradition?*, London, 1988, pp41-65.

‡ See J Bellamy Foster, *Marx's Ecology*, New York, 2000.

and their consequent relation to the rest of nature. Of course, we cannot here go either into the actual physical nature of man, or into the natural conditions in which man finds himself – geological, hydrographical, climatic and so on. The writing of history must always set out from these natural bases and their modification in the course of history through the action of men. (D McLellan, ed, as above, p160)

At the beginning of *The Critique of the Gotha Programme* (1875) Marx attacks the formula, often carelessly repeated by Marxists today, that "labour is the source of all wealth":

Labour is *not the source* of all wealth. *Nature* is just as much the source of use values (and it is surely of such that material wealth consists!) as labour, which itself is only the manifestation of a force of nature, human labour power. (K Marx and F Engels, *Selected Works*, Vol 2, as above, p18)

In *Capital*, Vol 3, Marx writes:

From the standpoint of a higher economic form of society, private ownership of the globe by single individuals will appear quite as absurd as private ownership of one man by another. Even a whole society, a nation, or even all simultaneously existing societies taken together, are not the owners of the globe. They are only its possessors, its usufructuaries, and, like *boni patres familias*, they must hand it down to succeeding generations in an improved condition. (*Capital*, Vol 3, Moscow, 1966, p776)

In *Capital*, Vol 1, he writes:

Moreover, all progress in capitalistic agriculture is a progress in the art, not only of robbing the labourer, but of robbing the

> soil; all progress in increasing the fertility of the soil for a given time, is a progress towards ruining the lasting sources of that fertility. The more a country starts its development on the foundation of modern industry, like the United States, for example, the more rapid is this process of destruction. Capitalist production, therefore, develops technology, and the combining together of various processes into a social whole, only by sapping the original sources of all wealth – the soil and the labourer. (*Capital*, Vol 1, as above, pp474-475)

And in his analysis of alienated labour in the *Economic and Philosophic Manuscripts of 1844* Marx writes:

> Nature is man's *inorganic* body – nature, that is, insofar as it is not itself human body. Man *lives* on nature – means that nature is his body, with which he must remain in continuous interchange if he is not to die. That man's physical and spiritual life is linked to nature means simply that nature is linked to itself, for man is a part of nature.
>
> In estranging from man (1) nature, and (2) himself, his own active functions, his life activity, estranged labour estranges the *species* from man. (http://www.marxists.org/archive/marx/works/1844/manuscripts/labour.htm)

It is first and foremost through their labour that human beings relate to nature. The alienation of labour, therefore, produces human alienation from nature. In Marx and Engels's day this alienation manifested itself in the separation of town and country, the degradation of working people's environment through pollution and sewage and through the erosion and exhaustion of the soil – all of which issues they took up at various points. With the further development of capitalism in the 20th century many of these problems became more severe – for example the vast slums and shanty towns of Third World cities, the American dust bowls of the depression – while new problems emerged, such as the destruction of whole species, the destruction of rainforests, the danger posed by nuclear power, the threat to the ozone layer, and so on. However, the discovery and establishment as scientific fact of the problem of humanly generated climate change has made it clear that the contradiction between capitalism and nature has reached a point of extreme crisis.

The problem of climate change is neither a scientific nor a technical problem. What needs to be done is both known and relatively straightforward. There has to be a massive reduction in carbon emissions worldwide, which in turn involves switching from fossil fuels (oil, gas and coal) to renewable sources of power (wind, solar and tidal), an end to overwhelming dependence on the private car and other carbon-emitting transport, and a systematic programme of insulation and other measures to cut emissions from houses. Plus there must be an immediate end to the felling of the rainforests. Perhaps there may need to be a restriction or curtailment of economic growth.

If these things are not done there will be a steady escalation in extreme weather events taking a huge toll in human life (it is fairly clear that this is already happening). This will be accompanied by wider climate change with immense human and economic consequences.

Yet, despite these devastating consequences, none of the straightforward measures outlined above are being taken, for the simple reason that they conflict with the immediate interests of capital. First, many of the world's biggest corporations, such as ExxonMobil, BP, Shell and Toyota, have a vested interest in fossil fuel use.

Second, the international competition between states (on behalf their respective capitalists) means that the world's biggest carbon polluters – the US, China, Europe, India, etc – face each other as competitors and each fears that if it makes the needed cuts in emissions it will lose out to its rivals who will not reciprocate.

These two factors both derive from fundamental features of capitalism. Moreover, if it were to prove necessary to restrict or halt economic growth, this would be completely incompatible with capitalism, which is based on the competitive compulsion to grow. And if the predictable consequences outlined above occur under capitalism it is highly likely that the response of our rulers will be some combination of racism, war, dictatorship and fascism – the response of the Bush administration to Hurricane Katrina multiplied many times over.

Yet, whereas economic depression and war (by destroying capital) and repression (by lowering wages and raising profits) can function as "solutions" or "self-correcting mechanisms" of a kind to economic crises caused by the declining rate of profit, none of these options will resolve the problem of climate change.

We can therefore say that there is a rapidly intensifying contradiction between capitalist relations of production and the very survival of the human species and many other species as well, and this makes the achievement of socialism a real historical necessity.

In the *Communist Manifesto* Marx wrote of the class struggle ending "either in a revolutionary reconstitution of society at large, or in the common ruin of the contending classes". It was an extraordinarily profound insight but at the time it could be no more than an abstract theoretical conclusion. Seventy years later Rosa Luxemburg wrote:

> Friedrich Engels once said: "Bourgeois society stands at the crossroads, either transition to socialism or regression into barbarism." What does "regression into barbarism" mean to our

lofty European civilisation? Until now, we have all probably read and repeated these words thoughtlessly, without suspecting their fearsome seriousness. A look around us at this moment shows what the regression of bourgeois society into barbarism means. This world war is a regression into barbarism. The triumph of imperialism leads to the annihilation of civilisation. At first, this happens sporadically for the duration of a modern war, but then when the period of unlimited wars begins it progresses toward its inevitable consequences. Today, we face the choice exactly as Friedrich Engels foresaw it a generation ago: either the triumph of imperialism and the collapse of all civilisation as in ancient Rome, depopulation, desolation, degeneration – a great cemetery. Or the victory of socialism, that means the conscious active struggle of the international proletariat against imperialism and its method of war. (R Luxemburg, *The Junius Pamphlet*, 1915, http://www.marxists.org/archive/luxemburg/1915/junius/ch01.htm)

Today, after two world wars, the Holocaust, Hiroshima and the ongoing threat of nuclear annihilation and the imminent possibility of irreversible climate change the concrete forms of such "regression to barbarism" and "common ruin of the contending classes" are clear for all to see.

8. On human nature

In everyday life – in the media, in the family, with friends and workmates, in the pub and on the street – ie in the entirety of political discussion and debate outside the academic world, the most common argument against Marxism (and socialism in general) is that it fails to take account of human nature. So widespread is this argument at every level of society that it does not seem like a philosophical argument at all, but in reality it is – and a very important one. Antonio Gramsci says that the question "What is man?" is "the primary and principal question that philosophy asks". He continues, "Reflecting on it, we can see that in putting the question 'what is man?' what we mean is: what can man become? That is can man dominate his own destiny, can he 'make himself', can he create his own life?" (A Gramsci, *Selections from the Prison Notebooks*, London, 1982, p351)

And, of course, when people claim that Marxism goes against human nature, or that socialism will never work because of human nature, what they mean is that a society of equality and freedom, a society run by the mass of ordinary people in the interests of ordinary people, is impossible because of the inherent defects of human nature.

One of the reasons why this argument is so popular and accepted is that it is very old and has been taught and disseminated for centuries. Perhaps its original form was the doctrine of "original sin" which can be traced back to the Genesis story in the Bible and to teachings of St Paul and the early Christian Church. The Catechism of the Catholic Church sums it up as follows:

By his sin Adam, as the first man, lost the original holiness and justice he had received from God, not only for himself but for all humans. Adam and Eve transmitted to their descendants human nature wounded by their own first sin and hence deprived of original holiness and justice; this deprivation is called "original sin". As a result of original sin, human nature is weakened in its powers, subject to ignorance, suffering and the domination of death, and inclined to sin (this inclination is called "concupiscence"). (http://www.vatican.va/archive/ENG0015/__P1C.HTM)

This notion of basic human wickedness was used to reinforce the power of the church, which held the keys to salvation. Later, in the 17th century, the political philosopher Thomas Hobbes argued that in the "state of nature" there is a "war of all against all" and "every man is enemy to every man". "In such condition", he said, "there is continual fear, and danger of violent death; and the life of man, solitary, poor, nasty, brutish and short." To escape this people had to submit themselves to a sovereign power standing above society for "men have no pleasure, but on the contrary a great deal of grief, in keeping company, where there is no power able to over-awe them all" (Thomas Hobbes, *Leviathan*, 1651, chapter XIII).*

In 19th century Britain, with the advent of industrial capitalism, the key characteristic attributed to human nature tended, appropriately enough, to be greed rather than lust or violence. Capitalist economic theory, as developed by Adam Smith, David Ricardo, John Stuart Mill and others, took as its

* Hobbes was a defender of absolute monarchy at the time of the English Civil War but he has exercised a huge posthumous intellectual influence, including on Émile Durkheim and Talcott Parsons, two of the key figures in modern sociology.

starting point and basic assumption the rationally calculating, self-interested acquisitive individual or "homo economicus" (economic man). As Mill put it, political economy "is concerned with [man] solely as a being who desires to possess wealth". He proposed "an arbitrary definition of man, as a being who inevitably does that by which he may obtain the greatest amount of necessaries, conveniences, and luxuries, with the smallest quantity of labour and physical self-denial with which they can be obtained" (John Stuart Mill, "On the Definition of Political Economy, and on the Method of Investigation Proper to It", *London and Westminster Review*, October 1836).

This concept of "economic man" remains to this day the cornerstone of mainstream, ie capitalist, economics. Later in the 19th century the German philosopher Friedrich Nietzsche shifted back in the direction of Hobbes and made the fundamental characteristic of human nature "the will to power". He held that all human beings and all living creatures are motivated primarily by the desire to expand their power over all others. Such a view leads inexorably to the conclusion that society will always be dominated by an elite of the most powerful individuals and it is hardly surprising that it influenced the Nazis. However, it also underpins the work of a number of major sociologists such as Max Weber and the elite theorists Vilfredo Pareto and Robert Michels, and even had an influence on more radical-seeming figures such as Michel Foucault.

In the 20th century there were numerous attempts to establish some kind of "scientific" basis for seeing human nature as essentially aggressive, acquisitive and territorial. These included *On Aggression* by the ethologist Konrad Lorenz, which sought to generalise an aggressive instinct from bird behaviour to humans; the work of the palaeoanthropologist (one who studies human origins through fossils) Raymond Dart, who developed the theory that early humans were essentially "killer apes" – ideas popularised by Robert Ardrey in *African Genesis* and *The Territorial Imperative*; and the development of evolutionary biology and sociobiology by the likes of Richard Dawkins and E O Wilson, who stressed the determination of human behaviour by "selfish" genes.

Over the centuries all these religious, philosophical and "scientific" ideas have seeped into the popular consciousness via a multitude of channels – pulpits, schools, universities, newspapers, films, television and so on. To give just one example, Robert Ardrey's books are known to have influenced Stanley Kubrick, who made the blockbuster movies *2001: A Space Odyssey* and *A Clockwork Orange*.

However, there is another important reason why so many people accept this very negative view of human nature – it seems to correspond to and explain a good deal of their actual life experience: the politicians who talk left to get elected but turn to the right as soon as they are in office; the trade unionists who start out as rank and file militants and end up as highly paid officials doing cosy deals with the bosses; the experience of the shop steward who tries to stand up to management but feels let down by her fellow workers; the little betrayals and disappointments people suffer in daily life and the simple fact that most of the time many people seem indifferent to wider injustices and suffering; and especially the fact that a lot of the time people seem passive and accepting of oppression.

So how does Marxism answer this very popular argument? First, by showing that human nature, in the sense of average or typical human behaviour, like everything else in the universe, is always changing. "All history is nothing but a continuous transformation of human nature," says Marx in *The Poverty of Philosophy* (http://www.marxists.org/archive/marx/works/1847/poverty-philosophy/ch02c.htm).

Thus, for example, in the West the nuclear family (husband, wife and their children) is widely thought of as a "natural" institution, part of human nature. In reality, at different points in history people have lived in all sorts of different types of "family" such as extended families (nuclear family plus wider kin), polygyny (one husband, many wives), polyandry (one wife, many husbands) and loose pairing. Among the Nayar of Kerala in South West India young women took one formal husband but would actually have sexual relations with up to 12 "lovers" or temporary husbands, without there being any common residence or domestic economic unit. Likewise polyandry was practised in Tibet until the Chinese takeover in 1950-51 when it was prohibited. To the Nayar and the Tibetans these arrangements doubtless seemed as "natural" as monogamous marriage did to 19th century Americans.

In Ancient Greece slavery was a key institution and generally regarded as "natural". Aristotle, in his *Politics*, justified slavery as follows:

> But is there any one thus intended by nature to be a slave, and for whom such a condition is expedient and right, or rather is not all slavery a violation of nature?
>
> There is no difficulty in answering this question, on grounds both of reason and of fact. For that some should rule and others be ruled is a thing not only necessary, but expedient; from the hour of their birth, some are marked out for subjection, others for rule... Such a duality exists in living creatures, but not in them only; it originates in the constitution of the universe. (http://www.cleverley.org/areopagus/docs/aristotle/aribk1_4_6.html)

In the Middle Ages it was widely believed that the feudal order, with its kings, lords and serfs, was both natural and ordained by God. As the hymn put it:

The rich man in his castle
The poor man at his gate
God made them high and lowly
And ordered their estate

But by the time we get to America in 1776 the authors of the Declaration of Independence believe that "All men are created equal" and that this truth is "self-evident" (except, of course, for people with black skin who are *by nature* inferior).

Second, Marx showed that the main factor shaping these changes in human behaviour and what is seen as "natural" is the way people earn their living, ie how they produce their means of subsistence. Thus the Nayar family arrangements were shaped by the fact that they were a warrior caste within the traditional Hindu caste system with men frequently absent on military service; whereas the nuclear family came to the fore because of the way it suited the needs of industrial capitalism. Aristotle and the upper ranking Ancient Greeks thought slavery was natural because their way of life depended on the exploitation of slave labour – the same reason that applied in the Southern states of the US.

The same is true of the "nature" or character of individuals within the same society. One person is generous, another less so; one person is ambitious and desperate to claw their way to the top, another is content to take a back seat. One person gets violent when drunk, another becomes benign. Moreover the influence of material conditions, especially social relations, on people's nature is seen very clearly in the way the same individual changes as their circumstances change. Thus the ordinary worker who wouldn't cross a picket line gets promoted to a managerial post and turns into a scab or a rank and file trade unionist who becomes a union official and then a union leader changes from a militant to a moderate to an organiser of sell-outs. It is not that being a scab or a sell-out was their true nature all along but that in each case their behaviour was strongly conditioned by their social position.

As well as changes in human nature there are also important continuities. In the final analysis, of course, the whole of human nature has come into being historically; it has evolved over millions of years from primates that were not human and before that from animals that were not even primates or mammals. But, in terms of the timescale relevant to the achievement of socialism, there are many things which will not change significantly. For example, basic human anatomy evolved over about 2.5 million years through many stages and reached its modern form (*Homo sapiens sapiens*) about 100,000 years ago, since when it has remained substantially unchanged. Other constants include our universal need for air, water and food, clothing and shelter and our dependence on *social* labour to obtain these necessities and hence our economic, social and psychological dependence on other people; our reproductive and psychological need for sex and probably for affection, love and so on. The question, therefore, arises – within these constants of human nature are there certain characteristics, such as greed, aggression or an inbuilt preference for hierarchy as the likes of Nietzsche, Lorenz and Ardrey claim, which would make socialism impossible?

Marxists are able to answer no to this question with considerable confidence. In 1877 the American anthropologist Lewis Henry Morgan published his book *Ancient Society*, based on his field work among the Iroquois Native Americans. Marx and Engels studied his findings intently and concluded that they showed that prior to the division of society into classes there was a stage of human development which they called "primitive communism" characterised by the absence of private property (in the means of production), exploitation or division into rich and poor or the oppression of women. Engels presented their arguments on these questions in his famous book *The Origin of the Family, Private Property and the State* (1884). For decades mainstream historians, social scientists, anthropologists and ethologists dismissed Engels's work, claiming that hierarchy and male dominance were universal. But research in the second half of the 20th century by palaeoanthropologists such as Richard Leakey, archaeologists (studying prehistoric societies via their artefacts and material culture) such as V Gordon Childe and anthropologists (studying existing indigenous societies) such as Eleanor Burke Leacock, Richard Lee and Colin Turnbull have shown that Marx and Engels were right.

More than that they have shown that humans have lived in classless societies from at least 100,000 years ago, and possibly 2.5 million years ago, until the advent of agriculture about 10,000 years ago – for between 90 and over 99 percent of human history. During this period people lived as hunter-gatherers (foragers) in small nomadic bands of 30 or 40. Both hunting game and gathering were collective activities involving the whole group, usually with a certain, not very rigid, division of labour between the sexes with men doing most of the hunting and women most of the gathering. Since they neither grew crops nor built houses nor had pottery for storage it was not possible to accumulate property beyond what could be carried on their backs or a surplus over and above what was required for daily living. Thus no group or class of exploiters living off the labour of others could emerge. Only with the arrival of agriculture was such a surplus produced, which then led to the development of a class controlling that surplus and with it the labour of others and, through the creation of a state, running society as a whole.

Eleanor Burke Leacock, an outstanding Marxist and feminist who made a special study of the Montagnais-Naskapi foragers of Labrador, makes the following generalisations based on her own and many other studies:

> What is hard to grasp about the structure of the egalitarian band is that leadership as we conceive it is not merely "weak" or "incipient", as is commonly stated, but irrelevant... Personal autonomy was concomitant with the direct dependence of each individual on the group as a whole.
>
> In egalitarian band society, food and other necessities were procured or manufactured by all able-bodied adults and were directly distributed by their producers... There was no differential access to resources through private land ownership and no specialisation of labour beyond that by sex, hence no market system to intervene in the direct relationship between production and distribution... The direct relation between production and consumption was intimately connected with the dispersal of authority... The basic principle of egalitarian band society was that people made decisions about the activities for which they were responsible. (Eleanor Burke Leacock, *Myths of Male Dominance*, Chicago, 2008, pp138-140)

Similarly Richard Lee, who studied at first hand the !Kung San of the Kalahari Desert in southern Africa, comments:

> Sharing deeply pervades the behaviour and values of the !Kung foragers, within the family and between families, just as the principle of profit and rationality is central to the capitalist ethic, so is sharing central to the conduct of social life in foraging societies...
>
> The fact that communal sharing of food resources has been directly observed in recent years among the !Kung and dozens of other foraging groups...lends strong support to the theory of Marx and Engels that a stage of primitive communism prevailed before the rise of the state and the break up of society into classes...

A truly communal life is often dismissed as a utopian ideal, to be endorsed in theory but unattainable in practice. But the evidence for foraging people tells us otherwise. (R B Lee, *The !Kung San*, Cambridge, 1979, cited in J Molyneux, *Is Human Nature a Barrier to Socialism?* London, 1993, p18)

Moreover the replacement of this primitive communism by class-divided society did not take place easily. As Chris Harman observes:

The full change took place over a very long period of time – 4,000 or 5,000 years [from the beginnings of agriculture – JM] in the most studied case, that of Mesopotamia. And in most cases it never got this far, so that even a century and a half ago millions of people were still living in non-class agricultural societies. (C Harman, "Engels and the Origins of Human Society", *International Socialism* 65 (winter 1994), p113)

What is being argued here is not the mirror image of the "people are naturally greedy" claim, ie that people are "naturally" unselfish. On the contrary human beings are capable of both selfish and unselfish behaviour and exhibit both characteristics in hunter-gatherer society and in capitalist society. Which type of behaviour predominates depends very much on social conditions, above all how production is organised and capitalist production is organised in a way that practically forces people to be selfish a lot of the time. However, what hundreds of thousands of years of egalitarian stateless foraging do prove, beyond reasonable doubt, is that there is no inbuilt factor in human nature which makes a society of freedom and equality impossible.

On the other hand, capitalism, while not incompatible with human nature (if it were it could never have existed) is most certainly very damaging to it. First it is very bad at meeting basic human needs. Despite immense and growing food production, it is estimated that in 2010 925 million people suffered from malnutrition, while over 880 million lacked access to clean drinking water. In the ancient city of Lagash in Sumeria in 2000 BC the average diet of an ordinary labourer was 2.4 litres of grain a day plus oil and beer, which works out in excess of 3,000 calories a day – well above the 2,500 calories recommended for an adult male and far better than the diet of most people in India or Sub-Saharan Africa today (see C Harman, as above, p124).

Secondly it alienates and distorts the most fundamental feature of human nature, that which made us human, namely our social labour, and in so doing threatens the very survival of the human race.

In conclusion it is worth noting that this Marxist reply to "the human nature argument" is not some ad hoc or improvised response to an unexpected or awkward objection. Rather it is based on all the fundamental elements of Marxist philosophy already outlined in this book: the basic dialectical idea that everything, including human nature, is changing, but that there is also continuity within that change; the materialist proposition that "social being determines consciousness" and therefore that human nature is shaped by social conditions, above all by production; that human nature as experienced under capitalism is really an alienation of human nature; and that the idea of human nature as basically greedy or aggressive is a key element in ruling class ideology which defends and justifies capitalism by trying to present its social relations as eternal and "natural".

9. Is Marxism a form of economic determinism?

If the charge of disregarding human nature is the most common everyday argument against Marxist philosophy, then the most common theoretical/academic criticism is that it is a crude economic determinism or mechanical materialism, or wrongly reduces all forms of oppression to class – these are all variations on the same theme.

Economic determinism

The criticism of Marxism that it "puts too much emphasis on the economic factor" is so popular with professional sociologists, historians, political philosophers and the like because it fits so neatly the needs of their social situation. Academics are people who earn their living, or like to believe they earn their living, on the basis of their ideas. Instinctively they are repelled by a theory which seems to downplay the role of ideas in history, and therefore to downplay the role of people like themselves. The professional ideologist is naturally drawn to theories which suggest that in the end it is the power of ideas that is decisive in shaping the world.

Within this there is a narrower career interest in theories that are "sophisticated" and "complex", and in questions "in need of more research and development" – so many research grants and publication opportunities – and a strong bias against definite answers of any kind. "Communism", the young Marx wrote, "is the riddle of history solved, and knows itself to be so," but such a claim would appal the typical academic who would much prefer the riddle to remain unsolved.

But if this explains the popularity of the objection we still have to assess its truth and on this I would start by saying that all talk of Marxism reducing everything to "economics" is inaccurate. Marx's theory of history, as *The German Ideology* makes clear, does not begin with "economics" or with "economic motives" but with human needs – both biologically determined and historically developed – and with the organisation of production to meet those needs.

> The first premise of all human history is, of course, the existence of living human individuals. Thus the first fact to be established is the physical organisation of these individuals and their consequent relation to the rest of nature... The writing of history must always set out from these natural bases and their modification in the course of history through the action of men. (K Marx and F Engels, *The German Ideology*, London, 1985, p42)

Nor does Marx claim that the organisation of production determines everything in history, merely that it constitutes a foundation or base on which everything else in history rests.

But isn't this a roundabout way of saying everything reduces to economics? No. The human needs we are talking about range from the very basic and absolute need for air, to the only slightly less pressing needs for drink, food, clothing, and shelter, to the need for social interaction (care, language, socialisation, etc) for babies to grow up human, the needs for love and sex (both a necessity for the survival of the species and a need felt by individuals) and "spiritual" needs for art, music, etc. Which of these needs can be called "economic"? In a sense none of them – is the need for air an "economic" need? At the same time without economics, ie the social organisation of production, none of these needs, except air, and even that may become problematic, can be met on a consistent basis.

What then is the relationship between this economic base of organised production and what Marx calls the "superstructure" of politics, law, philosophy, religion, art, etc? Clearly, as we have seen, economics is a necessary condition for the rest, but does it determine them in some mechanical or absolute sense? Not according to Marx, who mainly speaks of shaping or conditioning rather than strict determination: "The mode of production of material life *conditions* the social, political and intellectual life process in general" (my emphasis – JM) (D McLellan, ed, as above, p389) or Engels who was at pains to insist:

> According to the materialist conception of history, the *ultimately* determining element in history is the production and reproduction of real life. Other than this neither Marx nor I have ever asserted. Hence if somebody twists this into saying that the economic element is the *only* determining one, he transforms that proposition into a meaningless, abstract, senseless phrase. The economic situation is the basis, but the various elements of the superstructure – political forms of the class struggle and its results, to wit: constitutions established by the victorious class after a successful battle, etc, juridical forms, and even the reflexes of all these actual struggles in the brains of the participants, political, juristic, philosophical theories, religious views and their further development into systems of dogmas – also exercise their influence upon the course of the historical struggles and in many cases preponderate in determining their *form*. (Engels, Letter to J Bloch, 21 September 1890 in K Marx and F Engels, *Selected Works*, Vol 2, as above, p488)

The conditioning of the superstructure by the base is best understood, in my opinion, in terms of a combination of constraints and impulses.

First, the economic level of society constrains or sets limits to what is possible at the ideological or superstructural level. For example, modern art and modern culture generally are obviously impossible on a feudal or medieval economic base. Equally it was not possible to achieve modern political democracy – parliamentary government, universal suffrage, etc – without the development of capitalism with its cities and its working class.

Second, developments in the economic base create powerful impulses for change. For example the development of industrial capitalism into monopoly capitalism created a very powerful impulse towards imperialism, the division of the whole world between the great powers, and that in turn generated a huge pressure towards war. Thus the First World War was not an accident of history or mainly caused by ideology; on the contrary it had profound "economic" causes or, more accurately, causes located in the development of the forces and relations of production. At the same time it was by no means economically determined that world war would break out in August 1914 following an assassination in Sarajevo.

Similarly the victory of Nazism in Germany resulted from powerful "economic" impulses, specifically the severe crisis of capitalism and the need of the German capitalist class to find a way out of that crisis by crushing the working class and destroying all its independent organisations, rather than being caused by the German national character or the demonic oratory of Hitler (the two most popular "mainstream" explanations). But this did not make Hitler's triumph economically determined or inevitable. On the contrary political factors played a major role, particularly the failure of the two main parties of the working class – the Social Democrats and the Communists – to make common cause against the fascists, which permitted them to come to power without significant resistance. For a superb Marxist analysis of how and why this happened the reader is referred to Trotsky's writings of the time.*

Mechanical materialism

Economic determinism is an instance of mechanical materialism but it is also possible to reject economic determinism while retaining mechanical materialism. Thus human beings can be seen as so completely shaped and determined by social circumstances, not necessarily just economic, that the role of active human intervention in history is reduced to a minimum or disappears altogether. This kind of mechanical determinism can be found in various quarters ranging from the 17th century Dutch philosopher Spinoza through the 18th century French materialists (such as d'Holbach and Diderot) to the Marxists of the Second International such as Karl Kautsky and George Plekhanov and the so-called "dialectical materialism" of Stalinism.

But there is no justification for attributing mechanical materialism to Marx or Engels. One of Marx's earliest and most important philosophical works, the "Theses on Feuerbach" (1845) which Engels called "The first document in which is deposited the brilliant germ of the new world outlook" (F Engels, *Ludwig Feuerbach and the End of Classical German Philosophy*, as above, p3) begins precisely with a criticism of such materialism:

> The chief defect of all hitherto existing materialism – that of Feuerbach included – is that the thing, reality, sensuousness, is conceived only in the form of the *object* or of *contemplation*, but not as *sensuous human activity, practice*, not subjectively.

---

* See L Trotsky, *Fascism, Stalinism and the United Front*, London, 1989.

> Hence, in contradistinction to materialism, the *active* side was developed abstractly by idealism – which, of course, does not know real, sensuous activity as such. (D McLellan, ed, as above, p156)

"Idealism" here refers particularly to Hegel. And Marx returns to the issue in the third thesis:

> The materialist doctrine concerning the changing of circumstances and upbringing forgets that circumstances are changed by men and that it is essential to educate the educator himself. This doctrine must, therefore, divide society into two parts, one of which is superior to society.
>
> The coincidence of the changing of circumstances and of human activity or self-changing can be conceived and rationally understood only as *revolutionary practice*. (as above)

This emphasis, against both mechanical materialism and idealism, on the active role of human beings in making their own history runs throughout the work of Marx and Engels. In the *Economic and Philosophic Manuscripts of 1844* Marx writes that "the entire so-called history of the world is nothing but the creation of man through labour" (K Marx, *Early Writings*, as above, p166) and in *The Holy Family* Marx and Engels insist:

> *History* does *nothing*, it "possesses *no* immense wealth", it "wages *no* battles". It is *man*, real, living man who does all that, who possesses and fights; "history" is not, as it were, a person apart, using man as a means to achieve *its own* aims; history is *nothing but* the activity of man pursuing his aims. (http://www.marxists.org/archive/marx/works/1845/holy-family/ch06_2.htm)

In *The Eighteenth Brumaire of Louis Bonaparte* Marx

states, "Men make their own history, but they do not make it just as they please; they do not make it under circumstances chosen by themselves, but under circumstances directly encountered, given and transmitted from the past" (K Marx and F Engels, *Selected Works*, Vol 1, Moscow, 1962, p246). And in 1876 in *The Part Played by Labour in the Transition from Ape to Man*, the older Engels supplies the historical support for the young Marx's assertion that the history of the world is the self-creation of humans through labour.

The materialism of the 18th century met the philosophical requirements of the rising bourgeoisie in its need to develop natural science for the advancement of industry and its struggle against the aristocracy and its ally the Catholic Church. However, this materialism remained "mechanical" because this corresponded to the "mechanical" state of the natural sciences at this time* and because the class position of the bourgeoisie led them to view "the masses" as passive instruments of production, incapable of historical initiative and independent action.

Later mechanical materialism came to meet the needs of the reformist trade union and parliamentary bureaucracy of the Second International, who hoped and expected that the "objective historical forces" would deliver power into their hands but who rejected mass revolutionary struggle from below. Likewise it was admirably suited to the Stalinist bureaucracy who saw themselves (the party) as instruments of the historic process and the mass of workers as cogs in the machine of (state capitalist) accumulation.

The damaging political consequences of mechanical materialism have been seen on many occasions. Plekhanov and the Mensheviks' adherence to a rigid stages theory of the Russian

* See F Engels, *Ludwig Feuerbach and the End of Classical German Philosophy*, Peking, 1976, pp22-23.

Revolution – first a bourgeois revolution led by the bourgeoisie and later the struggle for socialism led by the working class – resulted in them first trying to hold back the struggle of the working class to the level acceptable to the bourgeoisie, and then in 1917 trying to substitute themselves for the missing democratic bourgeoisie, and then after October supporting the counter-revolution against the "premature" seizure of power by the Bolsheviks. This stages theory was then taken up by Stalin, in opposition to Trotsky's more dialectical theory of permanent revolution, and applied with disastrous effects in China in 1925-27 and Spain in 1936. Other important examples were the gradual slide of the German Social Democrats into parliamentary reformism under the cover of Kautsky's "orthodox" (ie mechanical) Marxism, which culminated in support for the German state in the First World War, and the catastrophic passivity of Italian Social Democracy in the "two red years" of 1919-20 and then in the face of rising fascism.

As can be seen from these examples there has been a persistent tendency for varieties of "Marxism" to lapse into mechanical materialism, a tendency which led Gramsci to observe that "the deterministic, fatalistic and mechanistic element has been a direct ideological 'aroma' emanating from the philosophy of praxis [Marxism], rather like religion or drugs" (A Gramsci, *Selections from the Prison Notebooks*, as above, p336). In my opinion this parallels the tendency of the leaderships of the working class movement to become bureaucratised and thus look down on the working class. And as Gramsci also notes, "when it [mechanical materialism] is adopted as a thought out and coherent philosophy on the part of the intellectuals, it becomes a cause of passivity, of idiotic self-sufficiency. This happens when they don't even expect the subaltern [the oppressed] will become directive and responsible" (as above, p337).

However, this tendency to mechanical materialism cannot be used as an argument against Marxism, (a) because in the final analysis it only reflects the pressure of bourgeois ideology and bourgeois conditions on the Marxist movement and (b) because bourgeois thought, as Lukács shows in *History and Class Consciousness*, continually oscillates between the poles of idealism and mechanical materialism and *only* authentic Marxism, standing on the ground of working class labour and struggle, is able to transcend this opposition.

Reductionism

A criticism of Marxism that became particularly widespread in the 1980s and 1990s is that Marxism is "reductionist". This related primarily to the issues of racism, sexism and homophobia and in each case it was claimed that Marxism was inclined to "reduce" these specific forms of oppression to the question of class oppression. What exactly was meant by these claims varied depending on context but in general there were four main allegations involved:

(1) That in the Marxist worldview these issues of oppression were considered unimportant, or of relatively little importance, compared to the central question of the class struggle.
(2) That the Marxist position is that solving the problems of racism, sexism and homophobia should wait until after the socialist revolution at which point they would be resolved "automatically".
(3) That the Marxist theoretical tradition had neglected these issues and failed to develop any serious theoretical account of them.
(4) That by failing to understand that racism, sexism and homophobia are each separate and autonomous issues (and struggles) and by trying to explain them as ultimately deriving from the class divisions in society, Marxism inevitably downgrades their significance.

In reply the first thing that should be said is that it is simply not true that the Marxist movement has ignored or treated as unimportant these issues of oppression. Obviously one can pick out examples of "Marxist" individuals or even parties that committed various sins of omission or commission on this score (by far the worst offenders have been Social Democrats of the Second International who supported imperialism, and the Stalinist rulers of the Soviet Union and other "Communist" countries who perpetrated innumerable crimes, but neither of these should be regarded as genuinely Marxist) but, taken as a whole, Marxism compares extremely favourably with any other political tradition or philosophy – be it liberalism, labourism, or anarchism.

On racism and national oppression, Marx and Engels actively supported the North in the American Civil War, defended the Indian Mutiny of 1857 and supported the struggles for Irish and Polish independence. Lenin and the Bolsheviks fought anti-Semitism in Russia (the main racism in that country) and defended the rights of oppressed nations to self-determination. Lenin led the field in Marxist opposition to imperialism and insisted that Marxists should actively support the anti-colonial struggle as well as working through the world communist movement to organise black and Asian workers internationally. The British Communist Party's first MP was the Indian, Shapurji Saklatvala, elected for Battersea in 1922 on a platform, among other things, of Indian independence. In the US both the Communist Party and the Trotskyists took the black struggle very seriously in the 1930s and 1940s and numbered in their ranks such outstanding anti-racists as Claude McKay, Paul Robeson and C L R James. C L R James and George Padmore, both Marxists, played a pioneering role in the African anti-colonial struggle. In Britain, from the 1960s to today, Marxists, both black and white, have played leading roles in the struggle against racism and fascism.

With regard to sexism Marx and Engels were both exceptionally advanced for their times and both committed to women's emancipation from the moment they became socialists. In his *Economic and Philosophic Manuscripts* Marx already put forward the idea that "From this relationship [of man to woman] one can therefore judge man's whole level of development" and in 1845 he approvingly quoted Fourier that "The degree of emancipation of woman is the natural measure of general emancipation" (quoted in Hal Draper, "Marx and Engels on Women's Liberation", *International Socialism* 1:44 (July/August 1970), p21). In the *Communist Manifesto* Marx and Engels proclaimed and defended "the abolition of the family". In 1884 in *The Origin of the Family, Private Property and the State* Engels produced the first historical materialist explanation of the origins of women's oppression, of "the world historic defeat of the female sex", as he called it. Eleanor Marx, Marx's daughter, was an activist among women workers in the East End of London and played a key role in supporting the Match Girls' Strike at Bryant & May in 1888, and in 1886, in "The Woman Question", wrote:

> The truth, not fully recognised even by those anxious to do good to woman, is that she, like the labour-classes, is in an oppressed condition; that her position, like theirs, is one of merciless degradation. Women are the creatures of an organised tyranny of men, as the workers are the creatures of an organised tyranny of idlers. (http://www.marxists.org/archive/eleanor-marx/works/womanq.htm)

Also in 1886, August Bebel, one of the principal leaders of German Social Democracy (when it was thoroughly Marxist), produced the very popular book *Woman: Past,*

Present and Future in which he defined socialism as "a society in which all the means of production are the property of the community, a society which recognises the full equality of all without distinction of sex" (quoted by Eleanor Marx, as above). Moreover the SPD built a powerful women's organisation and included such outstanding women leaders as Rosa Luxemburg and Clara Zetkin.

The Russian Revolution, in its early pre-Stalinist period, established full legal equality for women, including divorce and abortion rights (long before these were achieved in any Western capitalist society) and made an attempt to create the social infrastructure of crèches, nursery schools, communal restaurants and so on, needed to make formal equality a reality – an attempt frustrated, as was the revolution as a whole, by extreme economic collapse during the Civil War of 1918-21. Support for women's emancipation and the political organisation of women were established positions of the whole Communist International. In the 1960s and 1970s Marxist women played a significant part in the development of the Women's Liberation Movement and, broadly speaking, this has remained the case up to today. I know of no significant Marxist organisation or tendency in Europe or America which is not committed to women's equality and liberation.

With regard to homophobia the record might be seen as less impressive in that Marx and Engels shared some of the anti-homosexual prejudices of the period, but homophobia doesn't seem to have been a political issue at that time, ie there was, as yet, no movement or campaign of resistance to gay oppression. When in the 1890s German sexual reformers started to campaign against the anti-gay Paragraph 175 of the German Criminal Code they were supported by August Bebel and the (Marxist) SPD in the Reichstag, on the democratic grounds that consensual sexual behaviour was a private matter, and in 1895 Eduard Bernstein defended Oscar Wilde in the SPD's leading journal and attacked the view that homosexuality was unnatural. In 1897 it was an SPD member, Magnus Hirschfeld, who was the main mover behind the Scientific Humanitarian Committee – the world's first homosexual rights organisation.* The Russian Revolution, in December 1917 to be precise, abolished all Tsarist laws that that forbade or restricted homosexual activity. A 1923 pamphlet, *The Sexual Revolution in Russia*, stated the official Bolshevik position:

> Concerning homosexuality, sodomy, and various other forms of sexual gratification, which are set down in European legislation as offences against public morality – Soviet legislation treats these exactly the same as so-called "natural" intercourse. All forms of sexual intercourse are private matters. (Quoted in C Wilson, *Socialists and Gay Liberation*, London, 1995, p17)

These positions were immensely progressive for the time, ahead of anything achieved in the capitalist countries till very recently, but both the SPD and the Bolsheviks still tended to view homosexuality as an "illness" and this remained the dominant view among Marxists until the 1960s. (Stalinist Russia, however, recriminalised homosexuality in 1934.) What changed things was the emergence of the modern gay liberation movement after the spontaneous Stonewall riots in 1969 in New York. Since then the overwhelming majority of Marxists and Marxist organisations have come to reject any notion of homosexuality as illness and give active support to full LGBT equality and liberation.

This citing of the historical record is not, of course, a

---

* For a fuller account of this whole episode (including the weaknesses in the SPD's practice) see H Dee, *The Red in the Rainbow: Sexuality, Socialism and LGBT Liberation*, London, 2010, pp59-67.

philosophical or theoretical argument but it should be remembered that practice is the test of theory and Marxism's defence of the rights of people of colour, women and LGBT people and of other oppressed groups is not in the least accidental. Lenin expressed the point with characteristic force:

> Working class consciousness cannot be genuine political consciousness unless the workers are trained to respond to *all* cases of tyranny, oppression, violence, and abuse, no matter *what class* is affected...the Social-Democrat's [Marxist's] ideal should not be the trade union secretary, but *the tribune of the people*, who is able to react to every manifestation of tyranny and oppression, no matter where it appears, no matter what stratum or class of the people it affects. (V I Lenin, *What is to be Done?*, *Collected Works*, Vol 5, Moscow, 1961, pp412-423)

Moreover it should be stressed that it has *never* been the Marxist position that *any* group suffering oppression should wait for the revolution or for socialism. On the contrary Marxism has always advocated and supported resistance to oppression in the here and now, under capitalism, and argued that socialist revolution can only occur on the basis of, and as a result of, the coming together of a multitude of such struggles. Of course it is true that Marxism maintains that a complete end to all racism, sexism, homophobia, national oppression, etc is only possible with the abolition of capitalism and the end of class-divided society but that in no way implies any kind of passive waiting.

But what of the theoretical ability of Marxism to explain and understand the phenomena of racism, sexism and homophobia? I would argue that the Marxist method has proved a very powerful tool for the analysis of these and related issues.

In the first place the fundamental starting point of historical materialism that human beings differentiated themselves from animals through the production of their means of subsistence and created themselves and their history through labour dovetails with the findings of modern genetics that "races" in the biological sense do not exist and that humanity forms a single species (see S Rose, R C Lewontin, L J Kamin, *Not in Our Genes*, London, 1990, pp119-127) and thus denies racism any kind of "scientific" basis. As Chris Harman puts it:

> Racist arguments are wrong...because there is no backing for them in what we know about the genetic and biological make-up of living human beings. The human species cannot be divided into distinct sub-groups, each of which is made of individuals who are distinguished from those in other sub-groups by a complete set of genes and physical characteristics. At most it can be divided into groups according to variations in particular individual characteristics such as the amount of melanin in the skin, the tendency of hair to curl, eye colour, blood group, height, nose length, or whatnot. But these groups for particular characteristics are not congruent with each other... So the common sense notion of race...cannot be used as a valid scientific category. (C Harman, "Engels and the Origins of Human Society", as above, p186)

Secondly, Marx's theory of alienation argues that alienated labour leads also to alienation from our fellow human beings:

> An immediate consequence of the fact that man is estranged from the product of his labour, from his life activity, from his species being is the estrangement of man from man... In fact the proposition that man's species nature is estranged from him means that one man is estranged from the other, as each of them is from man's essential nature. (K Marx, *Economic and Philosophic Manuscripts of 1844*, London, 1981, p69)

This cuts to the heart of a key characteristic of racism and other oppressive ideologies – the tendency to dehumanise "the other" and regard their suffering as a matter of indifference.

Marx's analysis of the role of primitive accumulation of capital in the birth of capitalism also lays the foundations for an account of racism:

> The discovery of gold and silver in America, the extirpation, enslavement and entombment in mines of the aboriginal population, the beginning of the conquest and looting of the East Indies, the turning of Africa into a warren for the commercial hunting of black skins, signalised the rosy dawn of the era of capitalist production. These idyllic proceedings are the chief momenta of primitive accumulation. (K Marx, *Capital*, Vol 1, as above, p703)

Also, Marx analyses how capitalist competition not only affects the capitalists themselves but also tends to set workers against each other, to see each other as rivals for jobs, houses and other resources, unless it is combated by trade union and political organisation. These elements are brought together by Marx in a very insightful comment on the situation of the Irish in England:

> Every industrial and commercial centre in England now possesses a working class divided into two *hostile* camps, English proletarians and Irish proletarians. The ordinary English worker hates the Irish worker as a competitor who lowers his standard of life. In relation to the Irish worker he regards himself as a member of the *ruling* nation and consequently he becomes a tool of the English aristocrats and capitalists against Ireland, thus strengthening their domination *over himself*. He cherishes religious, social and national prejudices against the

> Irish worker. His attitude towards him is much the same as that of the "poor whites" to the Negroes in the former slave states of the US. The Irishman pays him back with interest in his own money. He sees in the English worker both the accomplice and the stupid tool of the *English rulers in Ireland.*
>
> This antagonism is artificially kept alive and intensified by the press, the pulpit, the comic papers, in short, by all the means at the disposal of the ruling classes. *This antagonism* is the secret of the *impotence of the English working class,* despite its organisation. It is the secret by which the capitalist class maintains its power. And the latter is quite aware of this. (K Marx, Letter to S Meyer and A Vogt, 9 April 1870, K Marx and F Engels, *Selected Correspondence*, Moscow, 1975, p221)

Since then many hands have contributed to the development of the Marxist analysis of racism. They include Leon Trotsky discussing black nationalism and socialism with the West Indian Marxist C L R James (who himself made a number of important contributions), and analyses of new world slavery by historians such as Eugene Genovese, Eric Williams and Robin Blackburn, of the anti-racist struggle in the US by Manning Marable and by Ahmed Shawki, of race and immigration in Britain by Paul Foot, and of the history of black people in Britain by Peter Fryer, as well as the work of Ambalavaner Sivanandan at the Institute of Race Relations and many others. Particularly useful in my opinion is the general framework put forward by Peter Alexander:

> Racism itself took shape in the course of the development of capitalism. As we shall see it has assumed three successive forms, the *racism of slavery*, the *racism of empire*, and *anti-immigrant racism*. (P Alexander, *Racism, Resistance and Revolution*, London, 1987, p6)

Alexander maintains that pre-capitalist societies, specifically ancient Greece and Rome and European feudalism, although full of brutal oppression and various prejudices, were not characterised by systematic racism in the way the modern world has been. He cites C L R James to the effect that:

> historically it is pretty well proved that the ancient Greeks and Romans knew nothing about race. They had another standard – civilised and barbarian – and you could have a white skin and be a barbarian and you could be black and civilised...the conception of dividing people by race comes with the slave trade. (C L R James, *Modern Politics*, Detroit, 1973, p124, quoted in Alexander, as above, pp5, 8)

Alexander also uses Peter Fryer's account of the rise of English racism in his magnificent *Staying Power: The History of Black People in Britain*. In brief, the argument is that the slave trade and new world slavery were established as part of the primitive accumulation of capital by the emergent British and European bourgeoisie, who were simultaneously engaged in their own struggle with the feudal aristocracy and absolute monarchies under the banner of "the rights of man". To reconcile the two they required the development of an ideology which, essentially, denied the common humanity of the slaves, positioning them as a separate and inferior "race".

After the abolition of slavery racism shifted somewhat to become, in the second half of the 19th century, a justification of empire, especially the British raj and the "scramble for Africa". Now the emphasis became not so much on the inhumanity of non-whites as their childlike character, which required them to be taken under the Western wing until such time (a long way off) as they reached sufficient maturity to govern themselves, as expressed in Rudyard Kipling's notorious poem "The White Man's Burden" (1898).

With the gradual passing of formal empire and the onset of large-scale immigration from the so-called "Third World", in Britain's case mainly from South Asia and the Caribbean in the 1950s and 1960s, the character of racism shifted again to an emphasis on alleged "cultural difference" and the danger of being "flooded" or "swamped" by an "alien invasion", as in the 1968 speeches of Enoch Powell and the infamous statement from Margaret Thatcher:

> If we went on as we are then by the end of the century there would be 4 million people of the new Commonwealth or Pakistan here. Now, that is an awful lot and I think it means that people are really rather afraid that this country might be rather swamped by people with a different culture and, you know, the British character has done so much for democracy, for law, and done so much throughout the world that if there is any fear that it might be swamped people are going to react and be rather hostile to those coming in. (Margaret Thatcher on *World in Action*, 27 January 1978)

This anti-immigrant racism was promoted by the ruling class and the media, as Marx suggested in his comments on anti-Irish racism, as a means of dividing and ruling over the working class and providing vulnerable scapegoats for social discontent.

To the three stages of racism identified by Alexander can be added a fourth, the racism of Islamophobia, which developed first in response to the Iranian Revolution of 1979, then as part of the West's identification of a new enemy after the "collapse of Communism", and then became greatly intensified as an ideological justification for the so-called "War on Terror" with its invasions of Afghanistan and Iraq. (Again Marxist and Marxist-influenced writers have been in the forefront of combating and analysing this phenomenon.[*])

On the specific case of anti-Semitism, which is a form of racism that has its own distinct history, Marxism has again proved capable of grasping its historical development and dynamic, most notably in the pioneering work of Abram Leon.[†]

And finally, on the closely related question of nationalism, which it is sometimes said Marxism neglects or cannot deal with, there are a number of valuable Marxist studies by, among many others, Lenin, Benedict Anderson, Eric Hobsbawm and Chris Harman.[‡]

In relation to women Engels's *The Origin of the Family, Private Property and the State* was pathbreaking not just as a distinctively Marxist analysis of women's oppression, but in terms of any kind of serious historical study of the question. Very briefly, what Engels argued was that anthropological evidence (drawn largely from Lewis Henry Morgan's *Ancient Society*) showed that the subordinate position of women was not inscribed in human nature, nor had it existed throughout human history; rather it had developed

---

* See for example C Harman, "The Prophet and the Proletariat", *International Socialism* 64 (autumn 1994), and L Fekete, *A Suitable Enemy*, London, 2009.

† A Leon, *The Jewish Question: A Marxist Interpretation*, New York, 1970. See also L Trotsky, "On the Jewish Problem", 1940, www.marxists.org/archive/trotsky/1940/xx/jewish.htm and J Rose, "Karl Marx, Abram Leon and the Jewish Question: a reappraisal", *International Socialism* 119 (summer 2008).

‡ See V I Lenin, *Critical Remarks on the National Question and the Right of Nations to Self-Determination*, Moscow, 1971, pp40-41; E Hobsbawm, *Nations and Nationalism since 1780*, Cambridge, 1990; B Anderson, *Imagined Communities*, London, 1991; and C Harman, "The Return of the National Question", *International Socialism* 56, autumn 1992.

relatively recently along with the emergence of private property and the division of society into classes, ie approximately 5,000 years ago. The relationship between class division and women's oppression was established through the institution of the male-dominated monogamous family which came into being to secure the inheritance of property and turned wives into the property of their husbands.

Later studies by Marxist anthropologists such as Eleanor Burke Leacock and Ernestine Friedl have confirmed Engels on this point and led to a clearer understanding of how male dominance emerged. Chris Harman offers the following explanation of how the basic gender equality that existed in hunter-gatherer societies gave way to male control of the surplus generated by class society and therefore to male dominance:

> The change was rooted in the new relations that grew up between people with the production of a surplus. The new intensive production techniques tended to prioritise men's labour over women's for the first time. Gathering, the main source of nutrition for hunter-gatherer societies, had been fully compatible with childbearing and breastfeeding. So had early forms of agriculture based on the hoe. But heavy ploughing and herding of cattle and horses were not. Societies in which women did these things would have low birth rates and stagnating populations, and lose out to societies which excluded most women from these roles... The plough... relieved women of the most exacting drudgery, but deprived them of the monopoly over the cereal crops and the social status which it conferred. Key decisions about the future of the household or lineage became male decisions, since it was males who would implement them. Other changes which accompanied the growth of the surplus had a similar impact. Women could engage in local trade, and there were cases of women playing a part in warfare. But long distance trade and

serious soldiering became male monopolies. Warriors and merchants were overwhelmingly male – and, as they increasingly exercised control over the surplus, ownership and power tended to become male prerogatives. (C Harman, *A People's History of the World*, London, 1999, pp29-30)

Identifying the origin of women's oppression in this way does not, however, explain why it continues even in modern society when it is plain that there is no biological basis at all for any significant division of labour between men and women, certainly not for a division that systematically favours men. The Marxist answer to this question has been that women's oppression continues because of the substantial benefits that the capitalist class and system derives from the institution of the family and from the division which it creates within the working class.

Capitalism, like every social system, has to ensure the refreshment, reproduction and rearing of labour power on a daily and generational basis. The institution of the family privatises this socially necessary task and makes it the responsibility of women, for whom it is supposed to be a "natural" obligation to be performed unpaid. This atomises the working class, dividing it into a multitude of separate and relatively isolated units, which has conservative effects ideologically and relieves the capitalist class of the need to pay for services it urgently requires. At the same time it is obvious that the capitalists benefit both economically and politically from having a substantial section of the working class pressured into working for lower wages and being socialised into passivity and social subordination.*

* For Marxist analyses of women's oppression today see L German, *Sex, Class and Socialism*, London, 1989, and J Orr, *Sexism and the System*, London, 2007.

This understanding of the crucial economic and ideological role of the family for capitalism also forms the foundation for the Marxist analysis of homophobia. Condemnation of homosexuality is based on two main arguments: (a) that it is "unnatural" and (b) that it "undermines the family". The first argument is extremely weak – on the one hand homosexual desire and experience is far too widespread to be considered contrary to nature and on the other nobody objects to a million and one other "unnatural" activities such as wearing clothes or flying in aeroplanes. Indeed these points were already made by the German Social Democrat Eduard Bernstein in his defence of Oscar Wilde in 1895.

Using the method of historical materialism he explained the way in which moral and sexual views were the product of definite historical and social circumstances. Bourgeois sexual morality was far from being the eternal and natural law that capitalism's hired moral hacks claimed. In fact it was a recent development and at that time was far from being universal. Precisely because attitudes to matters of sexuality are historically conditioned the yardstick of what was "natural" was invalid. Bernstein argued that the prevailing morality constituted the "normal" and that therefore deviations from it were abnormal rather than unnatural. Nature and norm were different things and most norms were, in any case, unnatural.

But although this "unnatural" argument is used ideologically to stigmatise homosexuality, the real driving force behind bourgeois homophobia is the second argument, the threat it represents to the family – or to be more precise the threat it represents to the *ideology* of the family, and the unequal gender roles embedded in it. In other words, it is not that LGBT equality would destroy the family by "tempting" everyone to become gay but that LGBT equality would undermine the claim that the male-dominated nuclear family is the ideal way to live.

Obviously it is not possible in the space available to give a full account of Marxist theory in relation to race, gender and sexuality but I think I have said more than enough to show that the charge of neglecting these issues or simply "reducing" them to class is false. Rather Marxism has used its theories of alienation, exploitation, class struggle and the materialist basis of ideology to explain concretely why and how racism, sexism and homophobia (and other prejudices) have arisen and persisted and why it is a necessity, not an optional extra, for socialism and human liberation that they are fought against and defeated by the working class movement.

But if Marxism has certainly dealt with these issues, perhaps some other theoretical standpoint or worldview has dealt with them better. The main challenge to Marxism in this area in recent years has come from what is known as "identity politics". Identity politics takes as its starting point not the working class as a whole or the working class as the liberator of humanity, but each individual or group's sense of their own social identity, usually defined in terms of race, ethnicity, gender or sexuality. The central claim of identity politics is that people can only speak authentically for themselves, that it is impossible to really understand racism, sexism, homophobia, etc unless one has been on the receiving end of it, and that therefore each of these groups (black people, women, LGBT people, etc) has to wage its own autonomous struggle for its emancipation.

This approach can have a strong emotional appeal but it is fatally flawed. In the first place "understanding" racism and so on is not just a matter of understanding its emotional impact but involves dealing with its history and its role in society as a whole. For example it is not possible to tell whether or not racism is natural simply by how it *feels*, and historical knowledge of black people or Jewish people is not specially given, or limited to, black people or Jews, as *Staying Power: The History of Black People in Britain* by (the white) Peter Fryer demonstrates.*

Secondly identity politics tends to generate unity where it is most damaging and undermine solidarity where it is most needed. Thus, because it tends to ignore or downplay class, it encourages cross-class unity of all blacks with Barack Obama or all women with Margaret Thatcher, ie unity of exploiter and exploited, which will certainly not be reciprocated, while it hinders unity and solidarity among the oppressed. Identity politics holds within itself a logic of division and fragmentation which does not stop at separating blacks from whites, or women from men: if black people have to struggle separately from whites and women separately from men what about black women, and then what about lesbian women as opposed to straight women or gay black men or lesbian black women or indeed Irish lesbian women and so on, more or less ad infinitum. For the purposes of building a career in academia or the media this categorising and tokenism can be useful to some individuals – perhaps the BBC needs to be seen to have a certain number of black or Asian or women newscasters and so on – but for the purposes of social and political struggle it is disastrous.

The logic of numbers and social power is such that the vital struggle for black, women's and LGBT liberation cannot be waged successfully by each group on its own. The decisive advantage of Marxism is that, in theory and practice, it provides the framework for articulating the fight against racism, sexism and homophobia within the overall struggle of the working class for socialism – a society in which the very roots of these oppressions will be torn up.

---

* Paul Gilroy makes precisely this point in his introduction to *Staying Power*, as above, pxii.

10. Ideology and truth

As we have already seen, for Marx, the ideas people hold always have material roots. Ideas do not fall into people's heads from the sky, nor are they put there by God. Rather they are always a reflection of, and a response to, people's real conditions of existence.

> It is evident that in all these cases their ideas are the conscious expression – real or illusory – of their real relations and activities... Men are the producers of their conceptions, ideas, etc – real, active men, as they are conditioned by a definite development of their productive forces and of the intercourse corresponding to these, up to its furthest forms. Consciousness can never be anything else than conscious existence, and the existence of men is their actual life-process. (K Marx and F Engels, *The German Ideology*, in D McLellan, ed, as above, p164.)

Developing this idea further Marx argues that the dominant ideas in society at any particular point in time will be the ideas that express the interests of the economically dominant, or ruling class.

> The ideas of the ruling class are in every epoch the ruling ideas, ie the class which is the ruling material force of society, is at the same time its ruling intellectual force. The class which has the means of material production at its disposal, has control at the same time over the means of mental production... The ruling ideas are nothing more than the ideal expression of the dominant material relationships, the dominant material relationships grasped as ideas... The individuals composing the ruling class

> possess among other things consciousness, and therefore think. Insofar, therefore, as they rule as a class and determine the extent and compass of an epoch, it is self-evident that they do this in its whole range, hence among other things rule also as thinkers, as producers of ideas, and regulate the production and distribution of the ideas of their age: thus their ideas are the ruling ideas of the epoch. (as above, p176)

However, it is not only the dominant ideas which have a class basis; the same applies to critical and dissident ideas in society. "The existence of revolutionary ideas in a particular period presupposes the existence of a revolutionary class" (as above, p176). Indeed, for Marxism, all significant and worked out ideologies are, directly or indirectly, articulations of the interests of classes or fractions of classes. Thus in Section III of the *Communist Manifesto* Marx defines the various rival schools of "socialism" in terms of their class roots, so we get feudal aristocratic socialism, petty bourgeois socialism and bourgeois socialism, and in the *The Poverty of Philosophy* he says of Proudhon, "He wants to soar as the man of science above the bourgeois and the proletarians; *he is merely the petty bourgeois*, continually tossed back and forth between capital and labour, political economy and communism" (K Marx, *The Poverty of Philosophy*, in D McLellan, ed, as above, p213). Marx does not mean by this that Proudhon is personally a petty bourgeois, but that his ideology represents the standpoint of the petty bourgeoisie.

And, of course, this logic applies to Marxism itself – it too has its material basis, it too expresses the interests of a definite social class. "Just as the economists are the scientific representatives of the bourgeois class, so the Socialists and Communists are the theoreticians of the proletarian class" (*The Poverty of Philosophy*, as above, p212). Again Marx doesn't just mean that he and Engels and other communists are "on the side" of the working class; he means that their ideas are a generalisation from the experience and struggle of the working class. "The theoretical conclusions of the Communists are in no way based on ideas or principles invented, or discovered, by this or that would-be universal reformer. They merely express, in general terms, actual relations springing from an existing class struggle, from an historical movement going on under our very eyes" (K Marx and F Engels, *The Communist Manifesto*, in D McLellan, ed, as above, p231).*

A number of important philosophical issues arise here. If the dominant ideas are bourgeois ideas and Marxist ideas view the world from the standpoint of the working class one could choose the latter over the former as matter of preference but how can either be said to be *truer* than the other? Are they not both equally biased? Would it not be more "scientific" to view the world objectively, from a neutral standpoint? This is the approach of many, perhaps most, in the academic world, especially those who consider themselves "social scientists". And did not Marx and Engels claim that their socialism was scientific, as in Engels's famous booklet *Socialism: Utopian and Scientific*?

The first thing to say is that in my experience the large majority of academic or mainstream social scientists who proclaim their neutrality are anything but. Not only do they have political and theoretical opinions and personal biases like the rest of us, but they are often quite open about them – indeed their students are often well aware of these preferences and know they are likely to get better marks if their work caters to

---

* In *What is the Real Marxist Tradition?*, as above, pp19-30, I show how the principal ideas of Marxism derive from the social being of the working class.

them. It is not that the professors and academics concerned are hypocrites and liars; it is just they do not recognise their biases to be such. Ideology is at its most powerful when it passes for common sense.

But this is not the fundamental problem. No matter how hard and how genuinely these academics and social theorists try to achieve a neutral standpoint they will fail. This is not only because as human beings they cannot completely escape their social conditioning and emotions but, crucially, because such a neutral standpoint does not exist to be attained. As Lenin put it:

> There can be no "impartial" social science in a society based on class struggle. In one way or another, *all* official and liberal science *defends* wage-slavery, whereas Marxism has declared relentless war on that slavery. To expect science to be impartial in a wage-slave society is as foolishly naive as to expect impartiality from manufacturers on the question of whether workers' wages ought not to be increased by decreasing the profits of capital. (V I Lenin, *Collected Works*, Moscow, 1977, Vol 19, p21)

We all, university professors or dock workers, top economists or unemployed single parents, live in a class-divided society. To achieve a truly neutral outlook on society would require finding a vantage point outside of society, outside of the world. That is not possible. This does not, however, mean that all standpoints are equal – the Marxist position is that its standpoint, the standpoint of the proletariat, is far superior, in terms of arriving at a true understanding of both history and present society, to the standpoint of the bourgeoisie or indeed that of the petty bourgeoisie.

This is because the proletariat and those who adopt its standpoint are engaged in a struggle to change society and therefore have a vital interest in understanding it, in laying bare how it works, how it has changed in the past and how it can be changed in the present. The effort to change the world to meet fundamental human needs has been the foundation of knowledge since *Homo habilis* first began to fashion tools or hunt game. The fact that to free itself the proletariat needs to change not just this or that aspect of capitalism but the system as a whole reinforces this. In contrast the standpoint of the bourgeoisie is the standpoint of a class which is trying to preserve existing society and therefore to prevent critical understanding of it. It has to pretend to itself and to the world at large that capitalism is a timeless eternal system. It can no more face up to the historical and transitory nature of capitalism than the feudal aristocracy could admit to itself in the 15th or 16th century that its time was up.

The bourgeoisie's whole social being blocks it from recognising either that its entire existence is dependent on the exploitation of the labour of workers or that capitalism rests on irreconcilable contradictions which drive it into crisis – each new crisis is always the result of some mistake or wrong policy or bad behaviour. Similarly the bourgeoisie cannot face up to the nature of its own state and its own law. It has to see them both as embodiments of "the national interest" or some similar formulation. Whereas the working class in struggle – in strikes, on picket lines, in factory occupations, on demonstrations and so on – has a pressing need to understand the real nature of the state and the law as they are continually being used against it.

The standpoint of the petty bourgeoisie – a class unable either to rule existing society or to change it – is an even worse foundation for understanding the world. Rather it lends itself to, on the one hand, the most unrealistic and utopian illusions about reconciling the classes and reforming the world on the basis of universal love and new age mysticism and, on the other hand, the most vicious and backward racist and fascist ideology.

The Marxist claim that the standpoint of the proletariat is the best vantage point for understanding the truth about society raises the age-old philosophical question (which goes back to Plato and Aristotle) of the meaning of "truth". There have been many theories of truth but the dominant theory, especially among materialists, is that "truth" means correspondence with fact or reality. Indeed for materialism, as was stated at the beginning of chapter 4, if a statement or theory is to be regarded as "true" it *must* correspond in some way to "reality". Moreover this "correspondence" theory of truth coincides with the main everyday usage of the word as in "Is this rumour I've heard true?" or "I swear to tell the truth" or "The truth is we are broke". And this is important because, as Wittgenstein argued, what words mean is determined by how they are used (though in a class society the meaning of certain ideologically loaded words can and will be contested).

Nevertheless there are certain difficulties with the correspondence theory. First, how do we know that a statement corresponds to reality? This applies particularly to statements that are not immediately verifiable by direct sense perception and also because sense perceptions can sometimes be misleading or deceptive. Second, once we move beyond very limited and everyday questions, "true" statements about the world only "reflect" or "correspond" to reality in certain aspects or to a certain degree, just as a photograph (a still flat image) can represent a scene or person accurately up to a point but cannot capture the richness and complexity of three-dimensional moving sensuous reality. Thus the statement that the earth is round is true relative to the statement that it is flat, but it is not absolutely true. The statement that "the shape of the earth is an oblate spheroid, a sphere flattened along the axis from pole to pole such that there is a bulge around the equator" is more true than the statement that it is round, but still not an absolute match with reality because of local topographical variations (mountains, hills, etc). Indeed there cannot be an exact correspondence between statement and reality because the exact shape of the earth is constantly changing, even in the time it takes to measure it or read or write the answer.

Marx cuts through these difficulties by insisting the question of truth is essentially a practical question. On the one hand, if an idea or theory works in practice this can only be because this idea or theory corresponds to certain aspects of reality – even though it does not, and cannot, give an exhaustive account of the whole of reality. Thus the fact that when Magellan set off to circumnavigate the world his ships did not fall off the edge but eventually ended up back in Portugal proves that the world is round rather than flat, even though "round" is a very rough approximation. On the other hand, as human practice expands so it presses against the limits of existing knowledge and reveals problems in existing theories. This leads to the development of new ideas and theories which in turn need to be tested and "proved" in practice. Thus there is a continual development: practice – theory – practice – theory – practice.

Lenin, commenting on Hegel in his *Philosophical Notebooks*, put it this way:

> Life gives rise to the brain. Nature is reflected in the human brain. By checking and applying the correctness of these reflections in his practice and technique, man arrives at objective truth. (V I Lenin, *Collected Works*, Vol 38, as above, p201)

But Lenin also expands on what he means by "reflection" so as to make clear it is not a simple or mechanical process:

> Cognition is the eternal, endless approximation of thought to the object. The *reflection* of nature in man's thought must be understood not "lifelessly", not "abstractly", *not devoid of movement, not without contradictions*, but in the eternal *process* of movement, the arising of contradictions and their solution. (as above, p195)

And, "human knowledge is not (or does not follow) a straight line, but a curve, which endlessly approximates a series of circles, a spiral" (as above, p363).

This, also, is how natural science develops. It does not at all consist of a simple accumulation of absolute truths but rather of a progressive series of approximations, of partial followed by more comprehensive explanations and "truths" or "laws" that apply within certain limits but not outside of those limits. Engels gives the example of Boyle's law.

> Let us take as an example the well-known Boyle's law. According to it, if the temperature remains constant, the volume of a gas varies inversely with the pressure to which it is subjected. Regnault found that this law does not hold good in certain cases...
>
> But Regnault, being a man of science...continued his investigations and discovered that in general Boyle's law is only approximately true, and in particular loses its validity in the case of gases which can be liquefied by pressure, namely, as soon as the pressure approaches the point at which liquefaction begins. Boyle's law therefore was proved to be true only within definite limits. But is it absolutely and finally true within those limits? No physicist would assert that. He would maintain that it holds good within certain limits of pressure and temperature and for certain gases; and even within these more restricted limits he would not exclude the possibility of

a still narrower limitation or altered formulation as the result of future investigations. (F Engels, *Anti-Dühring*, as above, pp111-112)

There is, however, an important distinction between natural science and social science. Both the natural and the social sciences are profoundly affected by capitalist society. In both spheres what issues arise, what gets investigated, which projects receive funding and which are ignored or swept under the carpet are matters shaped by the priorities of the system. Hence in the contemporary world there is a massive bias towards scientific research which has military implications, compared to medical or climate research. Nevertheless the bourgeoisie needs its natural science to work, even when the purposes to which it is put are deeply reactionary – B-52 bombers have to reach their target; nuclear missiles have to fire and explode to order – and therefore the science on which these things are based has to be true in the sense indicated above. Indeed there has been an alliance between the bourgeoisie and natural science, against the revealed religion of the Church and the feudal aristocracy, stretching back to the humanism of the Renaissance and the scientific revolution of the 16th and 17th centuries (Copernicus, Galileo, etc).*

Things stand quite otherwise when it comes to the study of society. Of course, the bourgeoisie needs all sorts of information, statistics, etc, but it does not need scientific understanding of society in the same way it does of nature. It is able to make profits perfectly happily without a scientific understanding of where profits come from, and it can rule society on the basis of its accumulated experience and class instincts ("instinct" here signifies internalised experience not

* For a brilliant brief analysis of this see F Engels, "Introduction to *Dialectics of Nature*", *Selected Works*, Vol 2, as above, pp62-80.

instinct in the biological sense). Since at least 1848 the principal function of mainstream social science has been legitimation of the existing order rather than being in any sense operational – and part of its role has been to discredit Marxist analyses of society.

Consider, for example, the question of social class – one of the fundamental questions of sociology. Despite looking at this issue for over 100 years, and despite the efforts of the likes of Max Weber, Émile Durkheim, Talcott Parsons, Robert Merton, John Goldthorpe, David Lockwood, Ralf Dahrendorf, Anthony Giddens and numerous others, mainstream sociology is no nearer a coherent or agreed theory of class and even the empirical studies on the question are decidedly limited. But this does not matter; it doesn't matter if most people, including most sociology students, are completely confused on the subject, so long as the dominant view (in education and in the media) is that the Marxist theory of class and especially the Marxist theory of the role of working class is "inadequate" or "out of date".

Similarly when it comes to history, it is a matter of secondary importance whether the prevailing interpretation of history is the liberal theory of progress, out and out empiricism or postmodern hostility to all grand narratives provided that historical materialism is rejected. The bourgeoisie acts, makes history, on the basis of its interests not on the basis of any of these theories but it would much prefer the working class not to be influenced or guided in its actions by the Marxist theory of history.

But the Marxist theory of history and analysis of society does arise out of real practical needs, the needs of the working class, and is focused on practice. It is a guide to action in the struggle to change the world and therefore is subject to the test of practice. On this basis Marxism's claim to be scientific is well founded and follows from, rather than being contradicted by, its character as the theory of the working class.

Does this mean that Marxism can claim to have been proved objectively true? Certainly there is an abundance of practical experience confirming many of the core propositions of Marxism: that capitalism generates massive inequality; that capitalism has a built-in tendency to economic crisis; that the survival of capitalism puts the survival of the human race at risk; that there is a fundamental conflict of interest between the capitalist class and the working class; that the state serves the interests of the capitalist class; that the working class, defined as people who live by the sale of their labour power, grows with the growth of capitalism. The evidence for these positions has not only been presented in numerous books but is written in the blood of working people the world over. The explanatory power of historical materialism, its ability to generate a rich and coherent account of history in all its complexity has also been demonstrated in many studies, including a number of undoubted masterpieces such as Marx's *The Eighteenth Brumaire of Louis Bonaparte* and *The Civil War in France*, Trotsky's *History of the Russian Revolution*, C L R James's *The Black Jacobins*, Geoffrey de Ste Croix's *The Class Struggle in the Ancient Greek World* and Chris Harman's *A People's History of the World*.

In one aspect, however, Marxism has not yet been proved true in practice and ultimately it is the most important aspect of all: the working class has not yet demonstrated in practice its ability to overthrow capitalism (more than temporarily and in limited areas) and liberate humanity by creating a classless society.

Does this create grounds for doubt? Clearly it does. Does it constitute grounds for rejecting Marxism? No, it does not. First, because the test of practice, on a question like this, cannot be subject to a restricted time limit. The defeat of the Paris Commune, the Russian Revolution, the German Revolution and the Spanish Revolution, etc were serious blows but they can be, and have been accounted for in Marxist terms, and they no more constitute proof of the historical incapacity of the working class than the failure of the bourgeois revolution in Renaissance Italy and 16th century Spain proved the incapacity of the bourgeoisie to overthrow feudalism.

Second, because the criterion of practice enters the debate here in another way. As human beings we are obliged, on pain of death, to act in and on the world. Stone Age foragers doubtless wanted the best available bows and arrows and stone axes but they were obliged to go out and dig tubers and hunt game with what they had, even if the outcome was not guaranteed, because the alternative was starvation. When a ship is sinking in the ocean there comes a time when you have to take to the lifeboats even if you are not certain of the way to reach land. This, increasingly, is the situation faced by the working class and by humanity. We are in a global crisis and we are heading for global catastrophe. We need to act. With the aid of which worldview, guided by which theory, should we try to change the world? In response to this question it can be said that Marxism has proved, in practice, again and again, that is by far the best available guide to action for the working class.

In terms of alternative guides to working class action there are really, on an international scale, only two: anarchism and social democratic reformism. Anarchism has always lacked a serious theoretical basis – there is simply no work in the anarchist tradition that can be set alongside *Capital* or even *The Communist Manifesto* or for that matter any of the works of history I cited above – and when it comes to its record in practice it has failed not only to win, but to come anywhere near winning as I have demonstrated elsewhere (see J Molyneux, *Anarchism: A Marxist Criticism*, London, 2011).

Social democratic reformism was theoretically refuted more or less as soon as it appeared in definite form, by Rosa Luxemburg in her *Social Reform or Revolution* (1900). Since then there have been a multitude of social democratic and labourite governments in countless countries round the world – Germany, France, Spain, Portugal, Italy, Greece, Sweden, Norway, Australia, New Zealand, Brazil and many others including no fewer than 11 Labour governments in Britain. Not one of these governments has made a serious attempt to challenge capitalism. In times of capitalist boom and prosperity they have sometimes provided limited reforms completely compatible with the survival and interests of the system. In times of crisis, as in Ireland at the moment of writing, or Greece until the Pasok government was deposed, they have invariably collaborated with the capitalist class in attacking the working class. As a "lesser evil" to be voted for, social democracy still just about survives. As a guide to working class struggle it has long departed the scene. That leaves Marxism as, in Jean-Paul Sartre's words, "the unsurpassable philosophy of our times".

11. Religion, morality and justice

The three topics treated in this chapter are clearly closely related. Religion is the most commonly encountered form of philosophy and is widely seen as the main source of morality, including by sociologists such as Émile Durkheim and Talcott Parsons. It is even suggested by some that without religion there can be no morality. The question of justice – of what is meant by justice and what would constitute a just society – is one the major issues in moral and political philosophy, and in everyday political life.

Religion

The statement that "religion is the opium of the people" is one of the best known of all Marx quotations but can also be one of the most misleading. This is because as well as pointing to the fact that Marx was an atheist and critic of religion it can also, taken in isolation, suggest or be used to suggest that Marx was a militant secularist – a sort of precursor of Richard Dawkins – for whom campaigning against religion was a key part of his political programme and who may even have been inclined to ban or "abolish" religion after the revolution. This is not only false, but has, as we shall see, very damaging political consequences.

However, let us begin with Marx's criticism of religion. Marx's scepticism about religion is evident from his very earliest writings such as the foreword to his doctoral dissertation on Epicurus in 1841 (see K Marx and F Engels, *On Religion*, Moscow, 1955, pp13-15), but his actual analysis of religion was first and most fully expressed in his introduction to *The Critique of Hegel's Philosophy of Right* in 1843, which was also the first work in which he identified the working class as the agent of revolution. At this time religion still had a powerful grip on society and on the popular consciousness but intellectually it had been seriously undermined by the French Encyclopaedists of the 18th century, such as d'Holbach and Diderot, and various young Hegelians like David Strauss and Ludwig Feuerbach. Marx takes their arguments against the truth of Christianity and religion in general more or less for granted, beginning, "For Germany, the *criticism of religion* has been essentially completed, and the criticism of religion is the prerequisite of all criticism" (K Marx and F Engels, *On Religion*, as above, p41). Then, drawing directly on Feuerbach's *The Essence of Christianity*, he argues, "The foundation of irreligious criticism is: *Man makes religion*, religion does not make man."

This is a devastating criticism of religion as a whole. If all religion is created by human beings, ie is a social product, and the differences between the teachings of the various religions and within religions over time are primarily shaped by the different social conditions under which each religion is formed and develops, then the truth claims of all religions are equally undermined. But instead of labouring this point for several hundred pages, in the manner of Richard Dawkins or Christopher Hitchens (who theoretically have not advanced beyond 18th century materialism on this question*) Marx moves immediately to the question of why human beings feel the need to create religion:

> Religion is, indeed, the self-consciousness and self-esteem of man who has either not yet won through to himself, or has

---

* For a Marxist critique of Dawkins and Hitchens see J Molyneux, "More than Opium: Marxism and Religion", *International Socialism* 119 (summer 2008).

> already lost himself again. But *man* is no abstract being squatting outside the world. Man is *the world of man* – state, society. This state and this society produce religion, which is an *inverted consciousness of the world*, because they are an *inverted world*. (as above, p41)

This is a reference to alienation – man who has "lost himself" – which we know was central to Marx's concerns at this time (the *Economic and Philosophic Manuscripts of 1844* were written in this year) and is the starting point of Marx's historical materialist analysis of religion. Human beings living in this society produce religion because, as I explained in chapter 3, they are alienated from their labour, the products of their labour and themselves and so live in a world which is out of their control and dominates them as an alien force even though they have made it themselves. Unable to understand this they imagine themselves ruled by a superior power or powers (god, gods, spirits, fate, etc) onto which they project their fears, hopes and aspirations.

Then, in a single sentence which contains enough ideas for several PhD theses, Marx outlines the many social functions performed by religion: "Religion is the general theory of this world, its encyclopaedic compendium, its logic in popular form, its spiritual *point d'honneur*, its enthusiasm, its moral sanction, its solemn complement, and its universal basis of consolation and justification" (as above, p41). This sentence, in itself, gives the lie to any idea that Marx put forward a simplistic, one-sided or "reductionist" theory of religion as merely a "tool of the ruling classes", though, of course, it has often been used in that way. Marx's next paragraph reinforces this point:

> *Religious* suffering is, at one and the same time, the *expression* of real suffering and a *protest* against real suffering.

> Religion is the sigh of the oppressed creature, the heart of a heartless world, and the soul of soulless conditions. It is the *opium* of the people. (as above, p41)

Seen in its context it is clear that the "opium of the people" phrase doesn't signify that Marx sees religion as only a top-down phenomenon by means of which people are fooled and manipulated but as both a means of reconciling people to the status quo and an expression of and protest against real suffering. This is crucial because history provides many examples of religion playing both these roles, often in opposition to one another within a given society.

Indeed this kind of division runs right through the history of Christianity. In the New Testament we are told both "Blessed are the poor in spirit, for theirs is the kingdom of heaven... Blessed are the meek, for they shall inherit the earth" and "Render unto Caesar that which is Caesar's", reflecting the fact that Christianity made the transition from being the religion of the poor within the Roman Empire to being the ruling religion of that empire. Then in the Middle Ages there was the dominant Church of Rome linked to the feudal aristocracy and the monarchs confronted by the heresies of the Cathars and Hussites, which reflected the first stirrings of the embryonic bourgeoisie, developing into the Protestant Reformation of Martin Luther. This, in turn, divided into the conservative Protestantism of Luther who crushed the peasants in the German Peasant War of 1525 and the revolutionary Protestantism of Thomas Münzer (see Engels's analysis of the role of religion in *The Peasant War in Germany* in *On Religion*, as above, pp98-118).

In recent times we have seen in apartheid South Africa the pro-apartheid Christianity of the Dutch Reformed Church versus the anti-apartheid Christianity of Bishop Desmond Tutu; in the US the anti-segregation, anti-racist Christianity of

Martin Luther King versus the conservative racist Christian right and in South America the reactionary pro-oligarch position of the Catholic hierarchy versus the radical sympathy with the poor of the "theology of liberation". Wherever there is class, national or ethnic conflict, especially where it is acute, both sides are likely to receive religious expression.

The conclusion Marx draws from this analysis is that, "The struggle against religion is, therefore, indirectly the struggle *against that world* whose spiritual *aroma* is religion" (as above, p41). Put simply, to get rid of religion you need to change the world so that people no longer need religion. Marx makes this point, completely missed by Dawkins and co, again and again in a flurry of different metaphors:

> The abolition of religion as the *illusory* happiness of the people is the demand for their *real* happiness. To call on them to give up their illusions about their condition is to call on them to *give up a condition that requires illusions*. The criticism of religion is, therefore, *in embryo, the criticism of that vale of tears* of which religion is the *halo*.
>
> Criticism has plucked the imaginary flowers on the chain not in order that man shall continue to bear that chain without fantasy or consolation, but so that he shall throw off the chain and pluck the living flower... It is, therefore, the *task of history*, once the *other-world of truth* has vanished, to establish the *truth of this world*. It is the immediate *task of philosophy*, which is in the service of history, to unmask self-estrangement in its *unholy forms* once the *holy form* of human self-estrangement has been unmasked. Thus, the *criticism of Heaven* turns into the *criticism of Earth*, the *criticism of religion* into the *criticism of law*, and the *criticism of theology* into the *criticism of politics*. (as above, p42)

Having shown how "the criticism of Heaven turns into the criticism of Earth" and "the criticism of politics", which shortly becomes the criticism of political economy, Marx has finished with religion philosophically and theoretically. Although his subsequent work is peppered with religious allusions and metaphors, he never returns to religion as a theoretical issue in its own right.*

What remains therefore is to draw out the implications of Marx's analysis of religion for politics and revolutionary practice today. This is necessary because over the last couple of decades the question of religion in general and one religion in particular, Islam, has assumed a political significance that hitherto it seemed to be gradually losing.

The first point is simply that it follows from this whole analysis that genuine Marxism neither implies nor advocates any sort of ban on religion or religious worship either now or in a future socialist society. When this was proposed by followers of the French socialist Louis Blanqui in 1874 Engels dismissed the idea rather mockingly arguing that such a ban would be completely ineffective and that "persecution is the best means of promoting undesirable convictions" (as above, p143). Far from banning religion, Marxists argue that religion should be a private matter in relation to the state, and complete freedom of religion should prevail under both capitalism and socialism. This was also the policy of the Bolsheviks. Lenin spelt this out unambiguously:

---

* Engels deals with the subject more but this is primarily in passing in *Anti-Dühring* or in historical studies (such as *The Peasant War in Germany* or *On the History of Early Christianity* as above) where he develops and illustrates the idea of apparently religious movements as articulations of real material interests.

> Religion must be of no concern to the state, and religious societies must have no connection with governmental authority. Everyone must be absolutely free to profess any religion he pleases, or no religion whatever, ie, to be an atheist, which every socialist is, as a rule. Discrimination among citizens on account of their religious convictions is wholly intolerable. Even the bare mention of a citizen's religion in official documents should unquestionably be eliminated. (V I Lenin, "Socialism and Religion", in *Collected Works*, Vol 10, Moscow, 1965)

The only sense in which Marxists contemplate the elimination of religion is through its gradual withering away as a result of the disappearance of its underlying social causes – alienation, exploitation and oppression.

The second point is that Marxists do not base their assessment of conflicts, struggles and movements on their religious coloration but on the class and social forces that are involved, especially on who is the oppressor and who the oppressed. For example no serious Marxist would make their point of departure for assessing the Irish Easter Rising of 1916 the fact that its leaders and many of its participants were Catholics as opposed to the Protestant British. Anyone who judged Malcolm X on the basis of his reactionary and bizarre religious views (when he was a member of Elijah Muhammad's Nation of Islam he believed white people were devils created 6,000 years ago on the Isle of Patmos by the scientist Dr Yacub) rather than the fact that he articulated, perhaps more powerfully than anyone else, the rage of black Americans at 400 years of oppression, would be missing the point entirely.

In the present climate of powerful Islamophobia it is necessary to stress that this applies also and especially to so-called Islamist movements or struggles of people who happen to be Muslim. The Arab revolutions of 2011 –

Tunisia and Egypt followed by the uprisings and attempted revolutions in Libya, Bahrain, Yemen and Syria – are first and foremost popular uprisings against dictatorships and oppression, ie democratic revolutions (with the potential to become workers' revolutions) regardless of whether the people making these revolutions were Muslim or not, or Sunni or Shia or Sufi, and even though many of these same people may vote for the Muslim Brotherhood or other Islamic organisations. Even so-called "Islamic fundamentalist" and "terrorist" organisations like the Taliban and Al Qaeda are primarily driven by economic and political issues, above all general anger at Western imperialism, rather than by religious doctrine.*

From a Marxist standpoint the common claim that religion is the main cause of war and conflict is false both for the past and the present. In relation to the 16th century Engels writes:

> In the so-called religious wars of the 16th century, very positive material class interests were at play, and those wars were class wars just as were the later collisions in England and France. If the class struggles of that time appear to bear religious earmarks, if the interests, requirements and demands of the various classes hid themselves behind a religious screen, it little changes the actual situation, and is to be explained by conditions of the time in Germany. (K Marx and F Engels, *On Religion*, as above, p98)

And in relation to Ireland in the 20th century I have written elsewhere:

---

* For an excellent and path-breaking Marxist analysis of the rise of Islamism see C Harman, "The Prophet and the Proletariat", as above.

> The view that the conflict in Ireland was essentially or primarily about religion is both manifestly false and plainly reactionary. It is false even in terms of the declared statements and consciousness of the principal protagonists. If many, though by no means all, Republicans were Catholics, no Republican would have said (or believed) that they were fighting for Catholicism; they fought for an independent, united Ireland. Things were less clear on the Unionist side where religious bigotry played a much larger role; nevertheless the principal declared goal was a "national" one, namely remaining "British". Moreover, it is abundantly clear that behind these conflicting national aspirations lay not religious differences about the doctrine of transubstantiation or the fallibility of the pope but real economic, social and political issues of exploitation, poverty, discrimination and oppression. To see the conflict as basically about religion was reactionary because it fitted with the racist stereotype of the Irish as primitive and stupid (after all "we" gave up fighting about religion centuries ago) and helped to legitimise British rule as a neutral arbiter between warring religious factions. (J Molyneux, "More than Opium: Marxism and Religion", as above, pp62-63)

Similarly the Marxist view of the Israel/Palestine conflict is that it is not at all determined by religion. Quite apart from the fact the most of the original leaders on both sides were secularists and many were atheists, the real issues are imperialism, land and national oppression. It would not alter the fundamental attitude of Marxists to the situation, ie their solidarity with the Palestinians, if the Israelis were Buddhists and the Palestinians were Zoroastrians or vice versa.

A third point is that Marxists are in favour of secularism under both capitalism and socialism. But secularism (like for example the right to national self-determination) cannot be regarded as an absolute principle overriding all others, such as anti-racism and anti-imperialism. Here, as in other matters, the standpoint of totality – the overall interests of the working class and the revolution – is the decisive criterion. And it is necessary to realise that the ruling class is perfectly capable of deploying secularist (and feminist etc) arguments to justify imperialist war and occupation as was done in relation to the war on Afghanistan and the current threats being made against Iran.

Much of this debate has focused on the question of the hijab (and the burqa and other variant forms of Muslim dress). It follows from the Marxist commitment to freedom of religious belief and practice that what is at issue here is not what Marxists, or anyone else, want Muslim women to wear, but what they have a right to wear without legal, physical or social intimidation. It should be clear from the standpoint of totality that any attempt to ban, restrict or demonise the wearing of the hijab, etc, whether on secularist or feminist or any other grounds, plays into the hands of the racists and is, objectively, racist in itself in that it increases the social isolation of and pressure on Muslim women, while also probably encouraging hijab-wearing as a badge of identity.

From Marx's analysis of religion it follows that it is not necessary for all or the majority of workers to be won to complete secularism or atheism before there can be a workers' revolution or the beginning of the socialist transformation of society. On the contrary such a transformation of mass consciousness prior to mass revolutionary struggle is actually unlikely since, as Marx and Engels wrote in 1845, it is only through revolutionary struggle that the working class can rid itself "of all the muck of ages". It is true that religious ideas, in any form, are an obstacle to a scientific Marxist analysis of society. Nevertheless working people with religious beliefs should be welcome in the revolutionary movement and in revolutionary parties. Lenin, who was absolutely intransigent in his philosophical opposition to religion, was equally insistent on this point: "We must not only admit workers who preserve their belief in God into the Social Democratic party, but must deliberately set out to recruit them; we are absolutely opposed to giving the slightest offence to their religious convictions," making only the proviso that "we recruit them in order to educate them in the spirit of our programme, and not in order to permit an active struggle against it" (V I Lenin, "The Attitude of the Workers' Party to Religion", www.marxists.org/archive/lenin/works/1909/may/13.htm).

Thus it all comes back to Marx's original conclusion in 1844 that in order to overcome religion it is necessary to change the society that gives rise to it.

Morality

The close association of morality with religion has led to the widespread view that moral principles should be absolute and eternal. Even those philosophers who do not accept the idea of divinely revealed morals, such as Immanuel Kant, have often tried to deduce absolute moral principles by means of abstract reasoning.

Marxists, not surprisingly, have rejected the notion of absolute or eternal moral laws on the grounds that (a) all morals, like all ideas in general, are created by human beings in the course of their historical and social development and thus are shaped by the needs of society and social conditions at any given point in time; and (b) in class-divided society, where the division between classes, between exploiter and exploited, is a fundamental one and where the needs and interests of the exploiting class conflict with those of the exploited class, morality too will have a class character. There will be no "supra-class" morals.

Engels writes:

> We therefore reject every attempt to impose on us any moral dogma whatsoever as an eternal, ultimate and forever immutable ethical law on the pretext that the moral world, too, has its permanent principles which stand above history and the differences between nations. We maintain on the contrary that all moral theories have been hitherto the product, in the last analysis, of the economic conditions of society obtaining at the time. And as society has hitherto moved in class antagonisms, morality has always been class morality; it has either justified the domination and the interests of the ruling class, or ever since the oppressed class became powerful enough, it has represented its indignation against this domination and the future interests of the oppressed. (F Engels, *Anti-Dühring*, as above, pp114-115)

And Trotsky likewise:

> Whoever does not care to return to Moses, Christ or Mohammed; whoever is not satisfied with eclectic hodgepodges must acknowledge that morality is a product of social development; that there is nothing invariable about it; that it serves social interests; that these interests are contradictory; that morality more than any other form of ideology has a class character. (L Trotsky, J Dewey and G Novack, *Their Morals and Ours*, New York, 1973, p21)

The question of socially conditioned versus eternal moral principles can be examined in relation to two test cases. First, the best known and most historically influential example of a set of moral laws supposedly derived from God, namely the Ten Commandments.

Actually the problem of the historical character of these

Commandments is posed even before we look at their content in terms of which of innumerable different translations and versions of the Bible to use. Are we instructed not to covet our "neighbour's house" nor "our neighbour's wife", "nor his manservant, nor his maid servant, nor his ox, nor his ass, nor anything that is thy neighbour's" as instructed by the King James Bible of 1611? Or do we prefer, as urged by the Good News Bible of 1966, "Do not desire another man's house; do not desire his wife, his slaves, his cattle, his donkeys, or anything else that he owns"?

In reality, of course the socially conditioned and historical character of the commandment leaps out the moment we look at it, whichever translation is used. In both cases a society is presupposed in which a wife is her husband's property and the family has slaves or servants, not to speak of donkeys and asses. The same is true of most of the other commandments. The first, "I am the LORD thy God, who hast brought thee out of the land of Egypt, out of the house of bondage. Thou shalt have no other gods before me," is clearly a reference to a very specific historical situation in which the "one" god has many rivals, ie the Israelites are one embattled tribe among many each with its own god (which helps to explain Jehovah's proclaimed vengefulness, "for I the LORD your God am a jealous God, visiting the iniquity of the fathers upon the children to the third and the fourth generation of those who hate me"). The second commandment, "You shall not make for yourself a graven image, or any likeness of anything that is in heaven above, or that is in the earth beneath, or that is in the water under the earth," far from being a universal principle has been observed by almost no Christians.

Let us leave aside the declarations in favour of family values ("Honour thy father and mother" and "Thou shalt not commit adultery") and the six-day week ("Six days shalt thou labour"); the two commandments which would seem to have the best claims to universality are the sixth and the eighth, "Thou shalt not kill" and "Thou shalt not steal", but actually neither withstands closer investigation. Taken literally the former would clearly prohibit war but this cannot possibly have been its meaning at the time because the Israelites of the period were pretty warlike and this is repeatedly and explicitly endorsed by the same god who delivered the commandments, as in "And when the Lord thy God hath delivered it into thine hands, thou shalt smite every male thereof with the edge of the sword" (Deuteronomy, 20:13). However, if an exception is made for war then numerous other exceptions present themselves. Is it permissible to kill to prevent someone else (a child, a woman, many people) being killed? Is it permissible for the state to execute people and for what – murder, treason, stealing a sheep? Are police permitted to kill people who they suspect might be going to kill other people?

In other words what is presented as an absolute moral principle turns out, for the very people who claim to subscribe to it, ie the overwhelming majority of Jews and Christians today and throughout history, to be highly circumscribed and dependent on circumstances. Moreover, we know from history that people on opposed sides in wars, revolutions and the class struggle have had and will have radically different ideas on who has the right to kill whom and under what circumstances.

"Thou shalt not steal" fares no better as an "eternal truth". The idea of theft as wrong presupposes the idea of property as a right. As Engels points out, "From the moment in which private ownership of movable property developed, all societies in which this private ownership existed had to have this moral injunction in common" (F Engels, *Anti-Dühring*, as above, p114). But, as we have seen, private property is a relatively recent development in human history.

Moreover the dependence of the concept of theft on property means that what counts as "stealing" changes as the form of property changes. In a society where people can be "owned" as slaves they can also be stolen (or coveted as the tenth commandment puts it). In a society without ownership of persons this is meaningless – people can be abducted, ie taken against *their* will not their master's, but not stolen.

As it happens the question of the changing meaning of theft played an important role in the intellectual development of the young Marx towards socialism. This was in relation to the laws against the theft of wood introduced by the Rhineland Parliament and taken up by Marx in the *Rheinische Zeitung* in 1842. For centuries it had been regarded as a natural right by peasants that they should be allowed to gather fallen timber. Now it was being asserted that such fallen timber was the property of the landowner and gathering it constituted theft. This conflict between customary rights and the new law resulted in five out of six of the prosecutions for theft in Prussia being to do with wood, and Marx recalls that it was this issue which first led him to him to examine "material interests" and "economic questions" (K Marx, Preface to *A Contribution to a Critique of Political Economy*, in *Selected Works*, Vol 2, as above, p361). In fact the issue was symptomatic of the development of capitalist social relations in agricultural lands and part of a wider European process involving the enclosure of common land and clearances such as the Highland Clearances.

The class character of disputes over the morality of theft is very clear. It is expressed in the 18th century rhyme:

> The law locks up the man or woman
> Who steals the goose from off the common
> But leaves the greater villain loose
> Who steals the common from the goose

It is also evident in the fact that from the capitalist point of view workers occupying a factory are "stealing" it from its rightful owners, whereas from a socialist point of view the whole of capitalism is based on the legal "theft" of workers' labour time. And who would deny the moral right of the poor to steal from a supermarket to feed their hungry children? Obviously supermarkets, and capitalists in general, would.

The best known and most influential attempt to formulate, by abstract reasoning, a fundamental and universal moral principle is Immanuel Kant's "categorical imperative" which states, "Act only according to that maxim whereby you can, at the same time, will that it should become a universal law" (I Kant, *Grounding for the Metaphysics of Morals*, 3rd edn, Indianapolis, 1993, p30). On the face of it this is more plausible than the Ten Commandments precisely because it is abstract but the moment we try to test it in practice, ie to derive any concrete guide to action from it, we run into exactly the same kind of problems.

Thus the injunction not to kill would seem to follow from the categorical imperative in that one might certainly wish that no one would ever kill people. Unfortunately this is of little use in the many situations where people actually do face moral dilemmas about taking human life. For example one might want to grant the right to kill in self-defence but would that mean willing as a universal law that everyone attacked would kill in self-defence? Clearly not. Clearly it would be necessary to indicate the nature and degree of the attack unless we want people attacked by water pistols and pea shooters to kill their assailants. Also does it not depend on who the people are? What are we to make of the right of a slave to kill a slave owner about to flog him or a slave owner to kill a slave attacking him in the act of escaping? In other words the categorical imperative turns out, on examination, not to be a universal principle at all but subject to all the same problems, qualifications, considerations of social context and different class standpoints as the biblical commandment. Trotsky correctly judges that "in spite of the fact that it occupies a high position upon the philosophic Olympus this imperative does not embody anything categorical because it embodies nothing concrete. It is a shell without content" (L Trotsky, J Dewey, and G Novack, *Their Morals and Ours*, as above, p22).

This rejection of any notion of eternal or absolute moral truths has led to the accusation against Marxism that it is an amoral doctrine and particularly to the charge that it holds to the principle that "the end justifies the means", ie it is permissible to perpetrate all sorts of wicked deeds – murder, terrorism, theft, lying – to achieve the "end" of revolution or socialism. This argument was discussed and convincingly refuted by Trotsky in the above cited *Their Morals and Ours*. Trotsky made two main points. First that virtually all those who levelled this charge against Marxism themselves adopted it when it came to *their* ends and goals. (War is the most obvious example of this since war can only be justified in terms of the ends it may achieve – national defence, freedom, peace, etc. But those who reject the use of violence in politics need also, to be consistent, to reject all arms, armed forces, police, prisons and law courts, regardless of consequences.) Second, that "A means can be justified only by its end. But the end in its turn needs to be justified" (as above, p48). The "end" of revolution is itself a means to the further "end" of the liberation of humanity.

> That is permissible, we answer, which really leads to the liberation of mankind. Since this end can be achieved only through revolution, the liberating morality of the proletariat of necessity is endowed with a revolutionary character... Permissible and obligatory are those and only those means...

which unite the revolutionary proletariat, fill their hearts with irreconcilable hostility to oppression, teach them contempt for official morality and its democratic echoers, imbue them with consciousness of their own historic mission, raise their courage and spirit of self-sacrifice in the struggle. Precisely from this it flows that not all means are permissible. When we say that the end justifies the means, then for us the conclusion follows that the great revolutionary end spurns those base means and ways which set one part of the working class against other parts, or attempt to make the masses happy without their participation; or lower the faith of the masses in themselves and their organisation, replacing it by worship for the "leaders"... These criteria do not, of course, give a ready answer to the question as to what is permissible and what is not permissible in each separate case. There can be no such automatic answers. Problems of revolutionary morality are fused with the problems of revolutionary strategy and tactics. (as above, pp48-49)

However, it is not just a matter of anti-Marxists; a number of Marxists have argued that Marxism rejects any concept of morality and is right to do so or, alternatively, that Marxism suffers from an "ethical deficit" and needs supplementing by some kind of universal moral philosophy (perhaps drawn from Kant or Aristotle). I disagree with both these points of view.

First, it is clear that while Marx and Engels sometimes said that they did not "preach morality at all" (K Marx and F Engels, *The German Ideology*, as above, p247), explicit and implicit moral judgements permeate their writings from first to last. In *The Civil War in France*, his magnificent account of the Paris Commune, Marx exudes contempt and moral condemnation of Adolphe Thiers and other suppressors of the Commune. Here is a short extract from his lengthy vitriolic denunciation of Thiers:

> Never in his long political career has he been guilty of a single – even the smallest – measure of any practical use. Thiers was consistent only in his greed for wealth and his hatred of the men that produce it. Having entered his first ministry, under Louis Philippe, poor as Job, he left it a millionaire. His last ministry... exposed him to public taunts of peculation in the Chamber of Deputies, to which he was content to reply by tears – a commodity he deals in as freely as Jules Favre, or any other crocodile. At Bordeaux, his first measure for saving France from impending financial ruin was to endow himself with three millions a year... A master in small state roguery, a virtuoso in perjury and treason, a craftsman in all the petty stratagems, cunning devices and base perfidies of parliamentary warfare; never scrupling, when out of office, to fan a revolution, and to stifle it in blood when at the helm of the state; with class prejudices standing him in the place of ideas, and vanity in the place of a heart; his private life as infamous as his public life is odious. (K Marx, *The First International and After*, London, 1992, p194)

And he concludes:

> Working men's Paris, with its Commune, will be forever celebrated as the glorious harbinger of a new society. Its martyrs are enshrined in the great heart of the working class. Its exterminators history has already nailed to that eternal pillory from which all the prayers of their priest will not avail to redeem them. (as above, p233)

In *Capital* Marx writes of the capitalists' "were-wolf's hunger for surplus value" and their "monstrous exactions, not surpassed...by the cruelties of the Spaniards to the

American red-skins" (K Marx, *Capital*, Vol 1, as above, p233) and having given detailed accounts of the vicious exploitation of child labour Marx comments, "Capital is reckless of the health or length of life of the labourer... To the outcry as to the physical and mental degradation, the premature death, the torture of over-work, it answers: Ought these to trouble us since they increase our profits" (as above, p257). Nor are these passages in any way unusual or exceptional in Marx and Engels's work and the same could be said for Lenin, Trotsky and Luxemburg, who all embed passionate moral judgements in all their political and historical writing. Indeed a number of the core concepts of historical materialism are loaded with ineradicable moral implications – alienation, exploiters and exploited, oppressors and oppressed. "Exploitation" is not a scientific as opposed to a moral concept or a moral concept as opposed to a scientific one, but both simultaneously.

Moreover, as we have seen, in their polemics on this question both Engels and Trotsky counterpose to bourgeois morality not an absence of morality but proletarian morality:

> What morality is preached to us today? There is first Christian-feudal morality... Alongside these we find the modern-bourgeois morality and beside it also the proletarian morality of the future... Which, then, is the true one? Not one of them, in the sense of absolute finality; but certainly that morality contains the maximum elements promising permanence which, in the present, represents the overthrow of the present, represents the future, and that is proletarian morality. (F Engels, *Anti-Dühring*, as above, p115)

There is no inconsistency or confusion here and no need to resort to non- or pre-Marxist ethical philosophy for support. Morals are not absolute principles but socially conditioned and produced general guidelines shaping human behaviour. In the first place, ie in pre-class foraging or "primitive communist" societies they arise from the common or shared needs of people in that situation; they endorse behaviour that contributes to the survival and wellbeing of the clan (who are interdependent and have fundamentally common interests) and prohibit behaviour that damages it. For example forager morality promotes the sharing of the spoils of the hunt and not its private ownership or consumption.

With the division of society into exploiters and exploited, there emerge classes with fundamentally opposed needs and interests and consequently divergent and opposed morals. In contemporary society this means basically the morality of the bourgeoisie versus the morality of the working class. In this conflict Marxism subscribes to the morality of the working class just as it supports its economic and political interests, because within capitalism it is the working class that represents the interests of the vast majority of humanity and, ultimately, of the survival and development of humanity as a whole. Working class or proletarian morality is the highest morality historically possible at the present time and until the achievement of a classless society.

It is important that by working class morality what is meant is not an empirical average of what working class people do or think. Some working class men (and middle class men as well of course) are brutal domestic abusers; that doesn't make domestic violence morally acceptable from a Marxist viewpoint. But neither is it a set of rules attributed to or prescribed for the working class by Marx or Marxists. Rather it is an accumulation of values, norms and maxims historically developed by the working class in its struggle within and against capitalism and which Marxists then support and subscribe to.

An obvious example is the working class principle that you don't cross a picket line. This is clearly not a universally observed or supported rule within the working class – if it were there would be no need for picket lines – but the fact that it is a guideline accepted and "felt" as a "moral" principle by significant sections of workers well beyond the ranks of Marxists or socialists is a huge benefit in the class struggle.* Moreover "Never cross a picket line" was a not a principle developed by Marx or Marxists – I may be mistaken but I cannot recall any mention of picket lines and not crossing them anywhere in Marx – and then imported into the working class. On the contrary it was developed, in struggle, by workers themselves because it met their needs. Marx and Engels were proud of the fact that they were the first socialists to support strikes and trade unions but in no way did they invent them. Working class people got there themselves long before Marx.

Anti-racism is another example. Of course this a political principle but it is also a moral issue, as the language and tone in which racism is discussed makes clear. Again it was not invented or created by Marxism as is shown by the case of the black Chartist leader, William Cuffay, who was elected to the Chartist National Executive in 1842, and again it extends far beyond the ranks of conscious Marxists or socialists as any stroll through London will confirm. Anti-racism, as we have already stressed, is also far more widespread in the working class than it is in the middle class or the bourgeoisie. This is because anti-racism flows, not automatically as there is the pressure of racism being injected from above, but powerfully from the need for class unity in struggle.

The question of sexual morality is more complex and merits a longer discussion than it can receive here.

* Though, as with all such guidelines, there are certain rare exceptions where class-conscious workers and socialists do have to cross picket lines.

Nevertheless what today would be considered a progressive and relatively "liberated" attitude to sexual relations has its social roots in the practices and attitudes widespread in the working class. The Paris Commune, which was only marginally influenced by Marxism as such, provides excellent evidence of this:

> The Commune adopted the widows and children of all National Guards killed in the civil war and specifically included in its decree women who were not officially married and their children; this recognised the situation, common in working class Paris, of men and women living together with neither the blessing of the Church nor the sanction of the state. (S Edwards, ed, *The Communards of Paris, 1871*, London, 1973, p108)

The leading Communard Arthur Arnould commented at the time:

> This was perhaps one of the most audacious acts of the Commune for it radically cut through a moral question... This decree...puts a woman legally and morally on an absolutely equal footing with a man, placing things in a real moral position... The union of man and woman must be an act that is essentially free, accomplished by two responsible persons. (Quoted in D Gluckstein, *The Paris Commune: A Revolution in Democracy*, London, 2006, p32)

It should be noted that the contrast between bourgeois and proletarian morality, their morals and ours, is conscious and explicit. The bourgeois leader and butcher of the Commune, Thiers, states, "Christianity, which has done so much for society, compels the man to respect the weakness of the woman which is like that of a slave" (as above, p32) whereas a working class woman in a speech at a Commune Women's Club says, "Marriage, *citoyennes*, is the greatest error of ancient humanity. To be married is to be a slave... The matrimonial state is a perpetual crime against morality" (as above, p187).

In general working class morality, to which Marxism subscribes, emphasises the values of solidarity and unity – with other members of the working class, of course, but also extending to other oppressed and downtrodden people – as in "an injury to one is an injury to all". In contrast bourgeois morality stresses individual achievement and individual responsibility, which stops at the boundaries of the family, or when necessary the nation-state. As the class warrior Margaret Thatcher put it:

> I think we've been through a period where too many people have been given to understand that if they have a problem, it's the government's job to cope with it. "I have a problem, I'll get a grant." "I'm homeless, the government must house me." They're casting their problem on society. And, you know, there is no such thing as society. There are individual men and women, and there are families. (http://briandeer.com/social/thatcher-society.htm)

From the standpoint of working class morality bosses and bankers pursuing the accumulation of capital are greedy while workers fighting for higher pay are engaged in what Marx called "a necessary form of self-assertion" and "fighting for us all". From the standpoint of bourgeois morality the workers are greedy and the bosses deserve their wealth.

"A really human morality which stands above class antagonisms" (F Engels, *Anti-Dühring*, as above, p248) will become possible only in a classless society. What will this morality look like? In the *Communist Manifesto* Marx suggests that it will be characterised by "the free development of each...[as] the condition of the free development of all" and by the principle "From each according to his abilities, to each according to his needs". However, beyond these generalities, important as they are, it is very difficult to say – any more than we can specify the kind of houses people will live in or transport they will choose. What Engels writes about sexual morality applies more widely and is a suitable note on which to close this section.

> What we can now conjecture about the way in which sexual relations will be ordered after the impending overthrow of capitalist production is mainly of a negative character, limited for the most part to what will disappear. But what will there be new? That will be answered when a new generation has grown up: a generation of men who never in their lives have known what it is to buy a woman's surrender with money or any other social instrument of power; a generation of women who have never known what it is to give themselves to a man from any other considerations than real love, or to refuse to give themselves to their lover from fear of the economic consequences. When these people are in the world, they will care precious little what anybody today thinks they ought to do; they will make their own practice and their corresponding public opinion about the practice of each individual – and that will be the end of it. (F Engels, *The Origin of the Family, Private Property and the State*, in K Marx and F Engels, *Selected Works*, Vol 2, as above, p241)

Justice

All that has been said about the social development and class character of morality applies to the special case of justice, which is a concept where issues of economics, politics and morality are fused. It can be summarised here very briefly.

Throughout the history of class society justice has borne a dual character. On the one hand there is the justice of the powerful – the justice that must be seen to be done, the justice that criminals must brought to, that gives us Courts of Justice and Ministries of Justice and which serves as an ideological cloak for the ruling class's state. On the other, the demand for justice that is the perennial cry of the oppressed – "Justice for the Martyrs!", "Justice for Stephen Lawrence!", "Justice for Trayvon Martin!", "No Justice, No Peace!" Generally speaking these alternative views of justice have stood diametrically opposed to each other often at either end of a police baton or on either side of a prison door.

Despite this fact, and partly because of it, bourgeois political philosophy over the last four centuries has devoted considerable energy to the attempt to establish, by rational deduction, a just basis for state power. Historically this mainly took the form of social contract theory, as developed by Locke, Rousseau, Hume and others. Social contract theory maintained that the basis for a just social and political order lay in an original, or notionally original, agreement or contract between citizens and government or between the citizens themselves. When it was first developed this idea of a social contract was undoubtedly progressive, even revolutionary, because it was counterposed to the traditional rule of the feudal lord and the concept of rule by divine right of absolute monarchs.

Once the bourgeois revolution had been carried through and various forms of bourgeois democracy had come into being, social contract theory started to play a reactionary role legitimising bourgeois society and the capitalist state, and masking the realities of wage slavery. Neither capitalist society nor any other form of class society has ever actually been founded on the basis of some initial contract or agreement of its citizens and in capitalist society today what takes on the appearance of a contract between governed and governors, namely general elections, are a deception because parliament is not where real power lies. Real power is based on a very different contract, that between capital and wage labour, which is anything but voluntary because workers are economically forced to sell their labour power. Today therefore the idea of a social contract produces little more than apologetics.*

But should Marx's conception of a fully developed socialist or communist society be seen as a conception of a just society? In my opinion it should not; rather it should be seen as a society *beyond* justice. It will be beyond justice, first, in the sense of being beyond, with the withering away of the state, any special apparatus of justice (police, courts, prisons, etc) and probably more or less beyond punishment as such.

---

* The major recent exponent of revamped social contract theory is the American liberal political philosopher John Rawls in his book *A Theory of Justice* (1971). Rawls attempts to formulate principles for a just society by trying to deduce them from the supposed deliberations of people in an imagined "original position" (a position in which they do not know who they are or what interests they have). For a Marxist critique of this theory which demonstrates that Rawls comes up with liberal capitalist answers because he builds liberal capitalist assumptions into his model from the start, see J Molyneux, "The Ideology of Justice: A Marxist Critique of Rawls", http://johnmolyneux.blogspot.co.uk/2012/05/ideology-of-justice-marxist-critique-of.html

In any case, in so far as punishment remains it will simply be the minimum necessary means of social self-defence, without any claims to be just, fair or "deserved". And, second, in the sense of being beyond any notions of "fair" wages or a "just" distribution of wealth. In *The Critique of the Gotha Programme* Marx attacks the whole idea of "just distribution" and of "equal rights" and concludes:

> In a higher phase of communist society, after the enslaving subordination of the individual to the division of labour, and therewith also the antithesis between mental and physical labour, has vanished; after labour has become not only a means of life but life's prime want; after the productive forces have also increased with the all-around development of the individual, and all the springs of co-operative wealth flow more abundantly – only then can the narrow horizon of bourgeois right be crossed in its entirety and society inscribe on its banners: From each according to his ability, to each according to his needs! (K Marx, *The First International and After*, as above, p347)

In the same text he also criticises the Gotha Programme for its stress on "distribution" arguing instead for a focus on the ownership and control of the "material conditions of production" (as above, p348).

The fundamental characteristic of the future communist society is, therefore, not justice but freedom and conscious human control.

12. Lukács, Gramsci, Althusser

Georg Lukács, Antonio Gramsci and Louis Althusser are without doubt the three most prestigious Marxist philosophers of the 20th century as far as the academic milieu is concerned. Any activist who so much as puts a foot inside a university social science or humanities department is likely to come across them. Consequently, although this book has dealt primarily with themes and issues rather than different philosophers, it does seem necessary to say something about them, even though it is not possible to do any of them justice in this short book.

What follows is simply an attempt to indicate briefly their main ideas and show how these relate to the basics of Marxist philosophy I have outlined.

Lukács

Georg Lukács (1885-1971) was a Hungarian philosopher who, following a period as a romantic anti-capitalist influenced by German idealist philosophy, especially Hegel, and the sociologist Max Weber, became a Marxist under the impact of the First World War and the Russian Revolution and joined the Hungarian Communist Party in 1918. He served as a member of the government in the short-lived Hungarian Soviet Republic (March to August 1919) and then, following its defeat, went into exile in Vienna. In 1923 he published a collection of essays entitled *History and Class Consciousness* which is widely regarded as the founding text of what has become known as "Western Marxism".

In 1924 Lukács wrote *Lenin: A Study in the Unity of his Thought* but he was denounced by leading Bolshevik Zinoviev as "revisionist" at the Fifth Congress of the Communist International. In 1928 he produced the so-called *Blum Theses* outlining a strategy for the overthrow of the Horthy dictatorship in Hungary, but this coincided with the advent of the extreme ultra-leftism of "Third Period" Stalinism and the *Blum Theses* were also condemned. At this point Lukács withdrew from active politics and devoted himself to research and literary criticism. From 1930 to 1945 he worked at the Marx-Engels Institute in Moscow where he managed, somehow, to survive Stalin's purges (which consumed the majority of exiled Hungarian Communists). In 1945 he returned to Hungary and participated in the Hungarian Communist government and in 1956 served in the brief liberalising government of Imre Nagy that accompanied the Hungarian Revolution. With the suppression of that revolution by Russian tanks Lukács barely escaped with his life but remained loyal to the Hungarian CP until his death, although he became increasingly critical of Stalin in his last years.

The problem with trying to offer any short account of Lukács's philosophy is that there were numerous different Lukácses at different times in his intellectual career. He engaged in various tactical retreats and capitulations in the face of Stalinism and his various philosophical shifts and self-criticisms seem to combine elements of both sincerity and expediency. Here I will deal only with the Lukács of *History and Class Consciousness*, by far his most important and most influential work, and the closely related *Lenin* study.

Lukács wrote *History and Class Consciousness* with two interconnected aims: to develop an interpretation of Marx that would critique and move beyond the mechanical materialism and economic determinism that characterised the Marxism of German Social Democracy and the Second International and to provide a philosophical foundation and justification for Bolshevism, ie the Leninist theory and practice of the revolutionary party.

This led him to focus on the role of proletarian consciousness in the revolutionary process. Lukács rejected any idea that the socialist transformation of society would be an automatic consequence of either the development of the productive forces or economic crisis and the collapse of capitalism:

> History is at its least automatic when it is the consciousness of the proletariat that is at issue. The truth that the old intuitive, mechanistic materialism could not grasp turns out to be doubly true for the proletariat, namely that it can be transformed and liberated only by its own actions, and that "the educator must himself be educated". The objective economic evolution could do no more than create the position of the proletariat in the production process. It was this position that determined its point of view. But the objective evolution could only give the proletariat the opportunity and the necessity to change society. Any transformation can only come about as the product of the – free – action of the proletariat itself. (G Lukács, *History and Class Consciousness*, London, 1971, pp208-209)

In his study of Lenin he puts it this way:

> Lenin's concept of organisation therefore means a double break with mechanical fatalism; both with the concept of proletarian class-consciousness as a mechanical product of its class situation, and with the idea that the revolution itself was only the mechanical working out of fatalistically explosive economic forces...the attitude of the proletariat itself, its determination and degree of class consciousness, by no means develops with fatalistic inevitability from its economic situation. (G Lukács, *Lenin: A Study in the Unity of his Thought*, London, 1970, p31)

Behind this emphasis on the non-automatic nature of proletarian class consciousness is Lukács's theory of "reification". Reification is the process by which "a relation between people takes on the character of a thing and thus acquires a 'phantom objectivity'" (G Lukács, *History and Class Consciousness*, as above, p83). This was based on Marx's analysis of commodity fetishism:

> A commodity is therefore a mysterious thing, simply because in it the social character of men's labour appears to them as an objective character stamped upon the product of that labour; because the relation of the producers to the sum total of their own labour is presented to them as a social relation, existing not between themselves, but between the products of their labour...it is a definite social relation between men, that assumes, in their eyes, the fantastic form of a relation between things. (K Marx, *Capital*, Vol 1, as above, p77)

And Lukács comments, "What is of central importance here is that because of this situation a man's own activity, his own labour becomes something that controls him by virtue of an autonomy alien to man" (G Lukács, *History and Class Consciousness*, as above, pp86-87). Here Lukács rediscovers and reintroduces into Marxism the theme of alienation which for 30 or more years had been buried, not only for Kautsky and Plekhanov but also for Lenin, Trotsky and Luxemburg; moreover he does so without having read the *Economic and Philosophic Manuscripts of 1844*, which were not published until 1930. He goes on to argue, "Reification is, then, the necessary, immediate reality of every person living in capitalist society" (as above, p197) and that the effect of reification and alienation is both to mask the realities of society, especially the reality of exploitation, and to induce in people an attitude of passive acceptance in the face of the "laws" of capitalist economics which appear as something beyond human control.* The bourgeoisie, Lukács maintains, are ideologically and practically unable to escape from this; their whole social being ties them to the logic of capital, ie the logic of capitalist competition and capital accumulation. Only from the standpoint of the proletariat is it possible to transcend and overcome reification.

However, the actual consciousness of most workers, says Lukács, is also profoundly affected by reification and this, along with the influence of bourgeois propaganda, is why many workers have such difficulty arriving at a clear understanding of their own class interests. "Thus the proletariat submits to the 'laws' of bourgeois society either in a spirit of supine fatalism...or else in a spirit of 'moral' affirmation (the state as an ideal, a cultural positive)" (as above, p196). Thus when it comes to defining class consciousness on which "the fate of the revolution (and with it the fate of mankind) will depend" (as above, p70) Lukács makes a sharp distinction between "true" class consciousness and "the sum [or] average of what is thought or felt by the single individuals who make up the class". Rather, "class consciousness consists in fact of the appropriate and rational reactions 'imputed' to a typical position in the process of production" (as above, p51).

This definition raises the issue of who is to decide what are "the appropriate and rational reactions" to be "imputed" to the proletariat. Lukács's answer is the Communist Party,

---

* Here it must be said that all of us who have lived through the global economic crisis of the last four years have been subject to the ceaselessly repeated mantra of the spokespersons of capitalism, faithfully echoed by social democrats and labourites, that there is no possible alternative to bank bailouts, cutbacks and austerity because no policy that goes against "the laws of the market" can even be seriously contemplated.

who are, in Lukács's words, "the tangible embodiment of proletarian class consciousness" (G Lukács, *Lenin*, as above, p27). "The Communist Party must exist as an independent organisation so that the proletariat may be able to see its own class consciousness given historical shape" (G Lukács, *History and Class Consciousness*, as above, p326). What enables the party to play this historical role as bearer of proletarian class consciousness is (1) its grasp of the "totality" of society by means of its correct theory (historical materialism); and (2) its internal discipline and its engagement of the whole personality of its members:

> Only through discipline can the party be capable of putting the collective will into practice... Every Communist Party represents a higher type of organisation than every bourgeois party or opportunist workers' party and this shows itself *in the greater demands made by the party on its individual members*. (as above, p316)

> The inner life of the party is one unceasing struggle against... its capitalist inheritance. The only decisive weapon it possesses is its ability to draw together all the party members and to involve them in activity on behalf of the party *with the whole of their personality*. (as above, p335)

In making an assessment of Lukács's philosophical contribution it is necessary to acknowledge, first, his deep knowledge and grasp of the Western philosophical tradition as a whole and of Hegel in particular; second, the correctness and necessity of his desire to make a root-and-branch theoretical criticism of the economic determinism and fatalism of the Marxism of the Second International; and third, the major importance of his reopening of the lost themes of reification and alienation which were, and remain, central both to the Marxist critique of capitalism and to the understanding of the role of human agency in transforming it. This last achievement in particular makes *History and Class Consciousness* one of the most significant contributions to Marxist philosophy in the 20th century.

However, in my opinion, it is also necessary to recognise that Lukács's position contains serious problems. His overall presentation of Marxism in *History and Class Consciousness*, with its overwhelming focus on consciousness (in the abstract) at the expense of more concrete analysis of the class struggle bears the stamp of his former idealism. Moreover his concept of "imputed" class consciousness provided by the party, while correct in its rejection of class consciousness as the simple average of what workers think at any one point in time, nevertheless underestimates the role of the working class itself, in struggle, in developing and creating this consciousness and the need for the party to learn from the class.

This in turn rests on and generates an idealised and elitist view of the revolutionary party. This appears in his conception of the party as involving "the whole personality" of its members. In reality in a mass workers' party this will not apply to large numbers of the party rank and file who have to work eight hours a day in a factory, office or call centre and have families, hobbies, etc, and who may join the party only in the midst of the revolution itself, but only to the "cadres" or top leaders (who Lukács, perhaps, views as *being* the party). Also his concept of the party as the embodiment of class consciousness leaves little or no room for an appeal from the party to the working class when the party is mistaken and/or lags behind the class. There is an interesting contrast here with Lenin who, in the course of 1917, frequently argued that the masses were to the left of the party and who in October 1917, when the Bolshevik Central Committee was dragging its feet over moving to armed insurrection, threatened "to go to the sailors!" (see V I Lenin, *Collected Works*, Vol 26, Moscow, 1972, pp74-85).

Lukács's latent idealism also appears in his view that Marxist orthodoxy consists exclusively of "method" and that it would not matter if "recent research had disproved once and for all every one of Marx's individual theses" (G Lukács, *History and Class Consciousness*, as above, p1). Clearly if it were proven, for example, that capitalism had overcome all its internal contradictions and that the proletariat had ceased to be the revolutionary class, Marxism as an overall theory would be refuted. This reduction of Marxism to method comes in the first and earliest essay of *History and Class Consciousness*, written in March 1919, and it is possible that he would not have used this formulation a few years later, but it remains indicative of a tendency in his thinking. The same can be said of his rejection of the dialectic of nature, which I discussed in the chapter on dialectics above, and which he repudiated in *Tailism and the Dialectic* written in 1925-26:

> Self-evidently society arose from nature. Self-evidently nature and its laws existed before society (that is to say before humans). Self-evidently the dialectic could not possibly be effective as an objective principle of development of society, if it were not already effective as a principle of development of nature before society. (G Lukács, *Tailism and the Dialectic*, London, 2000, p102)

Overall, Lukács's philosophical contribution can best be understood with the aid of Marx's First Thesis on Feuerbach, which I shall repeat:

> The chief defect of all hitherto existing materialism – that of Feuerbach included – is that the thing, reality, sensuousness,

> is conceived only in the form of the *object* or of *contemplation*, but not as *sensuous human activity, practice*, not subjectively. Hence, in contradistinction to materialism, the *active* side was developed abstractly by idealism – which, of course, does not know real, sensuous activity as such.

If the mechanical materialism of Kautsky and the Second International can be likened to the "hitherto existing materialism", Lukács can be seen as "the *active* side developed abstractly by idealism". Certainly compared to Marx, Engels, Lenin, Trotsky, Luxemburg and Gramsci, Lukács lacked prolonged and deep engagement with the "real, sensuous activity" of the working class movement and it showed in his philosophy.

Gramsci

Antonio Gramsci (1881-1937) was an Italian Marxist whose political and intellectual development ran, in some ways, parallel to that of Lukács. Like Lukács he was influenced in his youth by Hegelianism, particularly via the work of the leading Italian philosopher of the time, Benedetto Croce, and like Lukács he was won to revolutionary Marxism by the Russian Revolution and participated in the revolutionary struggles that, in Italy as in much of Europe, followed the First World War. During the "two red years" of factory occupations and factory councils in 1919 and 1920 Gramsci was closely engaged with the workers of Turin and edited the newspaper *L'Ordine Nuovo* ("New Order") which became the political expression of the factory council movement. In 1921 he took part in the foundation of the Italian Communist Party (PCI) as a breakaway from the Italian Socialist Party.

The defeat of the workers' occupations was followed by a wave of reaction culminating in the seizure of power by

Mussolini and the fascists. Gramsci went into exile in Moscow but then returned to Italy in 1924 as PCI leader, following a struggle against the dogmatic, "ultra-left" Amadeo Bordiga. However, he was soon arrested by the fascist state and sentenced to 20 years in prison. Prison conditions destroyed Gramsci's already fragile health and by the time of his release he was terminally ill. He died in 1937. But it was in his writings while in prison, known as the *Prison Notebooks*, that he made his most important and famous contributions to Marxist philosophy.

The *Prison Notebooks* are a fragmentary and very wide-ranging body of work dealing with topics as diverse as the Renaissance, modern Italian theatre and American Fordism – it is not possible to offer here even a brief summary of their contents. However, their most important theme, in my judgement, is Gramsci's reflections on the causes of the defeat of the revolution in Italy and in Europe following the Russian Revolution and it is possible to outline his main ideas on this question.

Gramsci's observations can be divided into two interrelated categories: first an analysis of the objective differences between Russia and the West; second a critique of the subjective factor – the philosophy, ideology and practice of the leaders and parties of the European socialist movement.

Gramsci maintained that due to Russia's economic and social backwardness there was a substantially different relationship between the state and civil society from that which was characteristic of Western Europe.

> In Russia the state was everything, civil society was primordial and gelatinous; in the West, there was a proper relation between state and civil society, and when the state trembled a sturdy structure of civil society was at once revealed. The state was only an outer ditch, behind which stood a powerful

system of fortresses and earthworks. (A Gramsci, *Selections from the Prison Notebooks*, London, 1982, p238)

And:

In the case of the most advanced states..."civil society" has become a very complex structure and one which is resistant to the catastrophic "incursions" of the immediate economic element (crises, depressions, etc). The superstructures of civil society are like the trench-systems of modern warfare. In war it would sometimes happen that a fierce artillery attack seemed to have destroyed the enemy's entire defensive system, whereas in fact it had only destroyed the outer perimeter... The same thing happens in politics, during the great economic crises. A crisis cannot give the attacking forces the ability to organise with lightning speed in time and in space; still less can it endow them with fighting spirit. Similarly, the defenders are not demoralised, nor do they abandon their positions, even among the ruins, nor do they lose faith in their own strength or their own future. (as above, p235)

This, in turn, is linked to Gramsci's emphasis on "hegemony", ie the element of cultural, moral and intellectual leadership that accompanies the element of force in the ruling of society by an economically dominant class, and that enables that class to rule by consent as well as repressive power. "The supremacy of a social group manifests itself in two ways, as 'domination', and as 'intellectual and moral leadership'... A social group can, and indeed must, already exercise 'leadership' before winning governmental power (as above, p57).

For Gramsci, the overwhelming role played by the Tsarist autocracy in Russia combined with the relative social weakness and lack of development of the bourgeoisie meant that when the repressive forces of the state shattered (as they did in a few days in the revolution of February 1917) Russian capitalism became vulnerable to a rapid "frontal assault". In contrast the bourgeoisie in Western Europe, with its centuries of organic development, was far more ideologically and institutionally rooted in society and thus better able to resist direct attack.

This analysis had major implications for revolutionary strategy and tactics. It underpinned Gramsci's critique of Bordiga and his "leftist" tendency in the Italian Communist Party who opposed any united front against fascism (which they did not differentiate from "normal" forms of bourgeois rule), and his critique of the "theory of the offensive" espoused by the "left" of the German Communist Party and other ultra-left currents in the Communist International. Gramsci argued for what he called a "dual perspective" combining "the levels of force and consent, authority and hegemony...agitation and propaganda...tactics and strategy, etc" (as above, pp169-170) and involving the construction of alliances, which in Italy meant in particular an alliance between the proletariat in the northern cities and the southern peasantry (see his article "The Southern Question" in A Gramsci, *The Modern Prince and other writings*, New York, 1970). In this perspective Gramsci also focused on the role of intellectuals on the achievement and maintenance of ideological hegemony. He writes:

> Now the intellectuals interest us as a mass not only as individuals. It is certainly important and useful for the proletariat that one or more intellectuals, individually, adhere to its programme and doctrine, merge themselves with the proletariat and become and feel themselves an integral part of it... But it is also important and useful that a break of an organic kind, characterised historically, is

> caused inside the mass of intellectuals; that there is formed, as a mass formation, a left wing tendency, in the modern sense of the word, that is one which is oriented towards the revolutionary proletariat. The alliance between the proletariat and the peasant masses requires this formation. (as above, pp50-51)

But he puts even more stress on the creation of a layer of what he calls "organic intellectuals". He argues that every social class arising on the basis of "an essential function in the world of economic production, creates, together with itself, organically, one or more strata of intellectuals which give it homogeneity and awareness of itself" (A Gramsci, *Selections from the Prison Notebooks*, as above, p5), not only economically but also socially and politically. In the case of the bourgeoisie this includes industrial technicians, economists, lawyers, cultural experts, etc. The working class needs its own equivalent: worker militants who have a clear idea of the historical role of their class. It is necessary, he says:

> to work incessantly to raise the intellectual level of ever growing strata of the populace... This means working to produce elites of intellectuals of a new type which arise directly out of the masses, but remain in contact with them to become, as it were, the whalebone in the corset.
>
> This...necessity, if realised, is what really modifies the "ideological panorama" of the age. (as above, p340)

This whole strategy of a struggle for hegemony required, in Gramsci's view, the leadership of a radically non-economistic revolutionary party and so is accompanied in the *Prison Notebooks* by a philosophical critique of the economic determinism and fatalism which was common to both the Marxism of the Second International and the sectarian ultra-leftism of Bordiga and the "lefts" in the Communist International, and was also still a force in the Russian Communist Party.

This had arisen because in a period of defeat, "When you don't have the initiative in the struggle...mechanical determinism becomes a tremendous force of moral resistance." Real will cloaks itself in an "act of faith" and a belief in historical inevitability as "a substitute for the Predestination or Providence of confessional religions". But when circumstances change and the oppressed are called upon to take over the running of society "mechanicism...becomes an imminent danger" (as above, p336).

Gramsci identifies not only the passivity of the determinist view but also its inherent elitism – it reflects a lack of faith that the oppressed can lead or fight.

He goes on to reject the possibility, as did Marx in his Second Thesis on Feuerbach, of "an extra-historical and extra-human objectivity", seeing such an idea as "a hangover of the concept of God", and to argue that "objective" always means "humanly objective". Humanly objective knowledge is thus something that must be fought for and that can only be fully realised when the human race is unified in a classless society.

Likewise Gramsci rejects mechanical materialism's claim to scientific foresight:

> In reality one can "scientifically" foresee only the struggle, but not the concrete moments of the struggle, which cannot but be the results of opposing forces in continuous movement, which are never reducible to fixed quantities since within them quantity is continually becoming quality. In reality one can "foresee" to the extent that one acts, to the extent one applies a voluntary effort and therefore contributes con-

cretely to creating the result "foreseen". Prediction reveals itself thus not as a scientific act of knowledge, but as the abstract expression of the effort made, the practical way of creating a collective will. (as above, p438)

Gramsci shows how mechanical materialism dehumanises and de-revolutionises Marxism: dehumanises it, not in the bourgeois or sentimental sense, but in the sense of erecting it into an ahistorical doctrine which no longer takes as its fundamental premise real historical human beings; de-revolutionises it in the sense of being unable to grasp the significance of revolutionary practice and thus undermining revolutionary intervention and initiative.

For Gramsci "the philosophy of praxis is...an absolute humanism of history" (as above, p465). The combination of this philosophical approach with his direct and intimate involvement with the workers' struggles of the "two red years" enabled him to formulate the problem of the development of class consciousness differently from Lukács* but much more in line with Marx and Engels's analysis of consciousness in *The German Ideology* (which Gramsci could not have read at the time). Gramsci argued that the existing consciousness of the "average" worker, and of the working class as a whole, was a "multiple" or "contradictory" consciousness consisting of elements of "common sense" (often drawn from the past and from the influence of the dominant classes) and "good sense", based on practical experience and activity.

---

* Or the early Lenin of *What is to be Done?*, who spoke of introducing socialism into the working class "from the outside", a view he later revised. See J Molyneux, *Marxism and the Party*, London, 1978, p59.

> The active man-in-the-mass has a practical activity, but has no clear theoretical consciousness of his practical activity, which nonetheless involves understanding the world in so far as it transforms it. His theoretical consciousness can indeed be historically in opposition to his activity. One might almost say that he has two theoretical consciousnesses (or one contradictory consciousness): one which is implicit in his activity and which in reality unites him with all his fellow workers in the practical transformation of the real world; and one, superficially explicit or verbal, which he has inherited from the past and uncritically absorbed. (as above, p333)

The development of revolutionary class consciousness is therefore not a matter of "imputing" an externally developed doctrine but of working to shift decisively the balance between these contradictory elements – a process of clarifying and rendering coherent a new worldview, the seeds of which are already present in the working class. Intellectuals and theory play a necessary role in this but it is a two-way process; in order to teach, the "educator" has to learn from the class. This raises what Gramsci calls "a fundamental theoretical question":

> Can modern theory [Marxism] be in opposition to the "spontaneous" feelings of the masses? ("Spontaneous" in the sense that they...have been formed through everyday experience illuminated by "common sense" ie by the traditional popular conception of the world). It cannot be in opposition to them. Between the two there is a "quantitative" difference of degree, not one of quality. A reciprocal "reduction" so to speak, a passage from one to the other and vice versa, must be possible. (as above, pp198-199)

The need for a reciprocal, dialectical relationship between organisation and spontaneity, leaders and masses, party and class, is repeatedly emphasised by Gramsci:

> It must be stressed that "pure" spontaneity does not exist in history: it would come to the same thing as "pure" mechanicity. In the most spontaneous movement it is simply the case that the elements of "conscious leadership" cannot be checked, have left no reliable document. (as above, p196)

He rejects equally those (such as contemporary anarchists and autonomists) who counterpose mass spontaneity to Marxist leadership and those who adopt a disdainful attitude to it:

> Neglecting, or worse still despising, so-called "spontaneous" movements, ie failing to give them conscious leadership... may often have extremely serious consequences. It is almost always the case that a "spontaneous" movement of the subaltern classes is accompanied by reactionary movement of the right wing of the dominant class. (as above, p199)

Failure to give any conscious leadership to the spontaneous revolts, he argues, plays into the hands of the extreme right. In contrast Gramsci cites the work of his Ordine Nuovo group in Turin as an example of the correct relationship between spontaneity and leadership:

> The leadership given to the movement was both creative and correct. This leadership was not "abstract"; it neither consisted of mechanically repeating scientific or theoretical formulae, nor did it confuse politics, real action, with theoretical disquisition. It applied itself to real men, formed in specific historical relations, with specific feelings, outlooks,

fragmentary conceptions of the world, etc, which were the result of "spontaneous" combinations of a given situation of material production with the "fortuitous" agglomeration within it of disparate social elements. This element of "spontaneity" was not neglected and even less despised. It was educated, directed, purged of extraneous contaminations; the aim was to bring it into line with modern theory–but in a living and historically effective manner...the movement gave the masses a "theoretical" consciousness of being creators of historical and institutional values, of being founders of a state. (as above, p198)

And it must be stressed, precisely because it is often ignored, that all of Gramsci's ideas – on the failure of the Italian Revolution, the state and civil society, the question of hegemony, the critique of fatalism and economism, the nature of class consciousness, and the relation of spontaneity and leadership – converge in his analysis of the essential role of the revolutionary party, or "Modern Prince" as he calls it in reference to Machiavelli.

It is necessary to note that an assessment of Gramsci's work is complicated by the fact that the extremely warm reception given to him in the academic world in the 1970s and 1980s (and still present to a considerable extent) was based on major distortion. On the one hand his originality was exaggerated in that the concept of "hegemony" was treated as Gramsci's own invention, as if earlier Marxists (Marx, Engels, Lenin, Trotsky, etc) had somehow been unaware of the fact that capitalist rule is never a matter of pure force but always includes an important ideological element. Indeed Gramsci himself attributed the idea of hegemony to Lenin: "The greatest modern theoretician of the philosophy of practice [ie Lenin] has in opposition to the various tendencies of 'economism'...constructed the doctrine of hegemony as a complement to the theory of the state-as-force" (quoted in C Harman, "Gramsci, the Prison Notebooks and Philosophy", *International Socialism* 114 (spring 2007), p106).

On the other hand, where Gramsci advocated a "dual perspective" of "force and consent", "domination and alliances", etc, academia tended to hear only "consent" and "alliances". In this way Gramsci was transformed from an intransigent revolutionary into an advocate of reformist "Eurocommunism" and even intellectual and cultural "struggle" quite separate from the actual movement of flesh-and-blood workers. This matter is pursued in detail in Peter D Thomas's immensely thorough study, *The Gramscian Moment*, where he comments, "The conversion of an unrepentant Communist militant...into a harmless gadfly is surely among the most bizarre and distasteful episodes of recent intellectual fashion" (P D Thomas, *The Gramscian Moment*, Leiden, 2009, p57fn) and by Chris Harman in *Gramsci versus Reformism* (London, 1983).

Setting this distortion aside, Gramsci's thought is not without its problems, notably the ambiguities, and sometimes contradictions, in the (often military) metaphors and analogies he uses to discuss the relations between state and civil society. It is very difficult to be sure how much these imprecisions derive from his need to conceal his meaning from the prison censor, from his use of an idiosyncratic personal shorthand, or from real lack of clarity in his ideas.* Also in his criticisms of mechanical materialism he sometimes uses formulations which permit idealist interpretations, such as his assertion that popular belief "that the external world is objectively real...is of religious origin... Since all

* For a detailed analysis of these difficulties see P Anderson, "The Antinomies of Antonio Gramsci", *New Left Review* 100, 1976.

religions have taught and do teach that the world, nature the universe were created by God before the creation of man, and therefore man found the world all ready-made" (A Gramsci, *Selections from the Prison Notebooks*, as above, p441).* In opposition to this I have argued (in chapter 4 above) that popular belief in the reality of the external world is based on human experience and practice, as well as being confirmed by science.

Nevertheless he remains a hugely important contributor to the Marxist philosophical and theoretical tradition, who along with Lenin, Trotsky and Luxemburg – and more satisfactorily than Lukács – rescued Marxism from its mechanistic reformist degeneration and restored its active interventionist revolutionary core. His writings as a whole, and not just the *Prison Notebooks*, are exceptionally rich and suggestive, containing a multitude of philosophical, historical and strategic insights that are of great assistance in the struggle to understand and change the world. Chris Harman rightly describes Gramsci's account of revolutionary leadership as "a guide for every revolutionary who wants to contribute to building a hegemonic socialist movement in the 21st century" (C Harman, "Gramsci, the Prison Notebooks and Philosophy", as above, p119).

---

* Though it should be noted that Gramsci disagreed with Lukács on the question of the dialectics of nature.

Althusser

As we have seen, Lukács and Gramsci developed as Marxists in the revolutionary wave that followed the Russian Revolution and the First World War. The French philosopher Louis Althusser (1918-90) was the product of a very different period. He was a member of the Communist Party of France (PCF) from 1948 onwards. This was a thoroughly Stalinised party – indeed the PCF was renowned for being one of the most Stalinist parties in Europe. What shaped Althusser's work was first and foremost the crisis in the international Communist movement signalled by the 20th Congress of the Communist Party of the Soviet Union in January 1956 (at which Soviet leader Khrushchev denounced the crimes of Stalin), the anti-Stalinist uprising in Hungary in October 1956 and the split between the Soviet Union and Maoist China which broke into the open in 1960-63. Althusser himself says:

> I would never have written anything were it not for the 20th Congress and Khrushchev's critique of Stalinism...but I would never have written these books if I had not seen this as a bungled destalinisation...a right wing destalinisation...my aim was to make a start on the first left wing critique of Stalinism. (L Althusser, 1975, quoted in G Elliott, *Althusser: The Detour of Theory*, London, 1987, p15)

However, as Perry Anderson has argued, "The real founding moment of Althusser's work was...the Sino-Soviet dispute" (P Anderson, *Arguments within English Marxism*, London, 1980, p107).

Khrushchev's denunciation of Stalin opened the gates to a flood of anti-Stalinist criticism both within Russia and Eastern Europe and within and around the Communist parties in the West. Much of this criticism was conducted under the banner of Marxist humanism, making extensive use of Marx's early writings and his concept of alienation. One thing, at least, seemed indisputable – in Russia and Eastern Europe people were still alienated. At the same time the Russian regime announced that Russia was in transition from socialism to full communism, that the dictatorship of the proletariat no longer existed and that the state had become the state of "the whole people".

Althusser was hostile to these developments but sympathetic to the radical rhetoric coming from China at the time of the so-called "Cultural Revolution". The Chinese leaders attacked the Russians for revisionism and defended the legacy of Stalin while adopting a seemingly more militant stand against US imperialism.

As a loyal member of the PCF, which was strongly pro-Moscow, Althusser declined to make direct political intervention in this dispute. Instead he opted to intervene at the level of philosophy via a theoretical critique of Marxist humanism. In two major works – a series of essays published as *For Marx* and a new interpretation of historical materialism (with Étienne Balibar), *Reading Capital* – Althusser insisted that Marxism was a "theoretical anti-humanism" which did not take as its starting point any concept of "human nature":

> One can and must speak openly of Marx's *theoretical anti-humanism*... It is impossible to *know* anything about men except on the absolute precondition that the philosophical (theoretical) myth of man is reduced to ashes. (L Althusser, *For Marx*, London, 1971, p229)

To sustain this proposition he argued that Marx's early writings, above all the *Economic and Philosophic Manuscripts of 1844*, were not part of Marxism proper because at this stage Marx had not yet freed himself from the influence of the (bourgeois idealist) Hegelian dialectic and the (bourgeois) humanism of Feuerbach. Rather, Althusser insisted there occurred a break – he called it an "epistemological break" – with the writing of *The German Ideology* in 1845.

> In 1845, Marx broke radically with every theory that based history and politics on an essence of man. This unique rupture contained three indissociable elements.
> (1) The formation of a theory of history and politics based on radically new concepts: the concepts of social formation, productive forces, relations of production, superstructure, ideologies, determination in the last instance by the economy, specific determination of the other levels, etc.
> (2) A radical critique of the *theoretical* pretensions of every philosophical humanism.
> (3) The definition of humanism as an *ideology*...
> This rupture with every *philosophical* anthropology or humanism is no secondary detail; it is Marx's scientific discovery. (L Althusser, *For Marx*, as above, p227)

The effect of this was to write the theory of alienation out of Marxism. Althusser calls the Marx of the *1844 Manuscripts* "the Marx *furthest from Marx*" and maintains that this theory is abandoned in Marx's mature "scientific" works, especially *Capital*.

Althusser also set out to minimise, contrary to Lukács, Gramsci and others, the extent to which Marx was indebted to Hegel and so rejected the view that the Marxist dialectic was a materialist inversion of the Hegelian dialectic or a discovery of "the rational kernel within the mystical shell" (K Marx, *Capital*, Vol 1, as above, p29). He argued that it was "*unthinkable that the place of the dialectic in Hegel's system could be conceived as that of a kernel in a nut*" or "*that the Hegelian dialectic could cease to be Hegelian and become Marxist by a simple, miraculous 'extraction'*" (L Althusser, *For Marx*, as above, p91). This was necessary for Althusser because he because wanted to reject both the Hegelian view of history as a development (in alienated form) of the Absolute Idea, and the view that history was made by (alienated) human beings. Instead he insisted that history was a "process without a subject" and that revolution rather than being the product of a central contradiction (between forces and relations of production or labour and capital) was the "overdetermined" outcome of multiple relatively autonomous contradictions or factors in which the economy is determinant only "in the last instance" (see the essay "Contradiction and Overdetermination" in L Althusser, *For Marx*, as above, pp94-128).

The phrase "in the last instance" is attributed by Althusser to Engels, but while Engels, as we have seen, rejects any mechanical economic determinism, he usually employs the stronger expression of "the economic movement finally asserts itself as necessary" (K Marx and F Engels, *Selected Works*, Vol 2, as above, p488). The consequence, it is fair to say, is an interpretation of historical materialism in which the autonomy of different structures (political, ideological, etc) is stressed and the role of the economy (ie of production) is considerably reduced, and in which what he calls "economism" (a tendency to overemphasise the role of the economy) is seen, along with humanism, as the besetting sin of both the Second International and much 20th century Marxism.

Althusser's opposition to humanism/economism made him hostile to any idea of "man making history". He preferred the propositions that "it is the masses who make history", which he ascribes to "Marxism-Leninism", and that "the class struggle is the motor of history", which he calls "the thesis of the

Communist Manifesto" (L Althusser, *Essays in Self-Criticism*, London, 1976, p46) and which, he argues, avoids the notion of a subject of history. "History therefore does not have a Subject, in the philosophical sense of the term, but a *motor*; that very class struggle" (as above, p99). It also led him to downplay the role of the forces of production relative to the relations of production. Whereas in traditional interpretations of historical materialism it was fundamentally the development of the forces of production that shaped or conditioned the relations of production, for Althusser this was "economism" and it was the relations of production (exploitation and class struggle) that were the key factor:

> The structure of the relations of production determines the places and functions occupied and adopted by the agents of production, who are never anything more than the occupants of these places... The true subjects...are therefore not these occupants or functionaries, are not "concrete individuals", "real men" – but *the definition and distribution of these places and functions. The true "subjects" are these definers and distributors: the relations of production.* (L Althusser, *Reading Capital*, London, 1970, p180)

A further innovation introduced by Althusser was a reconceptualisation of "science" and "ideology". The mature Marx, he argued, established a new science, "the science of the history of 'social formations'":

> To be more precise, I should say that Marx "opened up" for scientific knowledge a new "continent", that of history – just as Thales opened up the "continent" of mathematics for scientific knowledge, and Galileo opened up the "continent" of physical nature for scientific knowledge. (L Althusser, *For Marx*, as above, pp13-14)

For Althusser this science develops with considerable autonomy – it does not serve practice – and it is tested by its own internal procedures. He calls the activity of "doing" science "theoretical practice". And "if historical materialism is the science of history, dialectical materialism, Marxist philosophy, is the theory of scientific practice" (as above, p252).* It is science alone which generates "real" knowledge.

In contrast those concepts which he theoretically rejects – especially humanism and alienation – Althusser relegates to the status of "ideology". For Althusser "ideology...is distinguished from science in that in it the practico-social function is more important than the theoretical function (function as knowledge)" (as above, p231). Nevertheless ideology has a legitimate role to play in everyday life and politics as "the *lived* relation between men and their world, or a reflected form of this unconscious relation" (as above, p259). Indeed he argues:

> *So ideology is as such an organic part of every social totality.* It is as if human societies could not survive without these *specific formations...* Human societies secrete ideology as the very element and atmosphere indispensable to their historical respiration and life. Only an ideological world outlook could have imagined societies *without ideology* and accepted the utopian idea of a world in which ideology (not just one of its historical forms) would disappear without trace, to be replaced by *science...historical materialism cannot conceive that even a communist society could ever do without ideology*. (as above, p232)

* Althusser later revised this view of Marxist philosophy regarding it instead as "class struggle in the field of theory" (L Althusser, *Essays in Self-Criticism*, as above, p37) but I shall comment briefly later on Althusser's various "self-criticisms" and revisions.

Althusser then went on to formulate, as a development of the Marxist theory of the state, the concept of Ideological State Apparatuses. The Marxist classics, he argued, had focused on the repressive functions of the state apparatus but it was necessary also to examine how the state functioned to reproduce the social relations of production. This, he claimed, was achieved by means of Ideological State Apparatuses (ISAs) which "hail" or "interpellate" individuals as concrete subjects.*

> All the State Apparatuses function both by repression and by ideology, with the difference that the (Repressive) State Apparatus functions massively and predominantly by repression, whereas the Ideological State Apparatuses function massively and predominantly by ideology. (L Althusser, "Ideology and Ideological State Apparatuses", in *Lenin and Philosophy and Other Essays*, London, 1971, p136)

Althusser then enumerates what he considers to be the various ISAs – the churches, the education system, the family, the legal system, the political system (including political parties), the trade unions, the media and the cultural system. For a period in the 1970s this theory was one of the most influential of Althusser's ideas within the Anglophone academic world, where it was commonly associated with Gramsci's concept of hegemony.

Ever since it was first set out Althusser's version of Marxism has been the subject of intense controversy. Hugely influential in France in the 1960s and British universities in

---

* "Interpellation" is the idea that ISAs hail or summon individuals to play their allotted roles in the relations of production – as worker, supervisor, manager, etc – by giving them the illusion that they are the subjects or movers of this process.

the 1970s it has been defended and applied, at least for a time, by Étienne Balibar, Nicos Poulantzas, Barry Hindess, Paul Hirst and others, while being vigorously attacked by the likes of Lucien Sève, Jacques Rancière, E P Thompson and Chris Harman. Under fire Althusser made a number of modifications and retreats from his original positions; his strategy seems to have been to rebut his critics but to announce that he had discovered various errors or weaknesses himself. Thus charged with importing bourgeois sociological "structuralism" into Marxism he rejected the charge but admitted to being a "Spinozist"* and also to what he called "my theoreticist error" (L Althusser, *Essays in Self-Criticism*, as above, p119).

As in the case of Lukács, it is not possible in this highly compressed exposition for me to follow Althusser through his various "confessions" and reconsiderations which, taken together, effectively dismantled his own system, especially as it is the early Althusser who is the important Althusser. A thorough and conscientious account of the whole process is to be found in Gregory Elliott's *Althusser: The Detour of Theory*, which also offers a judiciously balanced assessment of Althusserianism.

My own view of Althusser, however, is much less "balanced" than Elliott's in that I regard virtually all his "innovations" and "developments" of Marxism as mistaken and his "system" as a whole as deeply Stalinist. I would share Chris Harman's characterisation of Althusser as the emperor who has no clothes (see C Harman, "The Emperor has no Clothes", *International Socialism* 125 (winter 2009)).

The first problem is simply that the Marxism of Marx is

---

* Baruch Spinoza, 17th century Dutch philosopher and pioneer of the radical Enlightenment.

not what Althusser says it is. It is not true that Marx progressively abandons the concept of alienation after the supposed break of 1845 or in his mature works in general. I will cite two brief quotations from *Capital*:

> As in religion man is governed by the products of his own brain, so in capitalistic production, he is governed by the products of his own hand. (K Marx, *Capital*, Vol 1, as above, p582)

> All means for the development of production transform themselves into means of domination over, and exploitation of, the producers; they mutilate the labourer into a fragment of a man, degrade him to the level of an appendage of a machine, destroy every remnant of charm in his work and turn it into a hated toil; they estrange from him the intellectual potentialities of the labour-process in the same proportion as science is incorporated in it as one independent power; they distort the conditions under which he works, subject him during the labour-process to a despotism the more hateful for its meanness; they transform life-time into working time... (as above, p604)

Many more passages could be cited. István Mészáros in *Marx's Theory of Alienation* offers decisive textual proof on this question, producing numerous quotations from all Marx's major economic works. In relation to the *Grundrisse* (1859) Mészáros writes, "This work contains hundreds of pages where the problems of alienation are analysed in a comprehensive way" (I Mészáros, *Marx's Theory of Alienation*, London, 1975, p224).

On the question of Marx's relation to Hegel and the "inversion" of the Hegelian dialectic Marx's statement on this is pretty clear and unequivocal:

My dialectic method is not only different from the Hegelian, but is its direct opposite. To Hegel, the life process of the human brain, ie, the process of thinking, which, under the name of "the Idea", he even transforms into an independent subject, is the demiurgos of the real world, and the real world is only the external, phenomenal form of "the Idea". With me, on the contrary, the ideal is nothing else than the material world reflected by the human mind, and translated into forms of thought.

The mystifying side of Hegelian dialectic I criticised nearly 30 years ago, at a time when it was still the fashion. But just as I was working at the first volume of *Das Kapital*, it was the good pleasure of the peevish, arrogant, mediocre Epigonoi [Büchner, Dühring and others] who now talk large in cultured Germany, to treat Hegel in same way as the brave Moses Mendelssohn in Lessing's time treated Spinoza, ie, as a "dead dog". I therefore openly avowed myself the pupil of that mighty thinker, and even here and there, in the chapter on the theory of value, coquetted with the modes of expression peculiar to him. The mystification which dialectic suffers in Hegel's hands, by no means prevents him from being the first to present its general form of working in a comprehensive and conscious manner. With him it is standing on its head. It must be turned right side up again, if you would discover the rational kernel within the mystical shell. (K Marx, *Capital*, Vol 1, as above, p29)

When Althusser rejects the idea that "man makes history" he counterposes to it what he calls "the Marxist-Leninist thesis" "It is the masses who make history", but he offers no citation or reference to either Marx or Lenin to back up this claim. Marx, however, did write in the *Eighteenth Brumaire* (a text after the claimed "break") that "Men make their own history, but not in circumstances of their own choosing".

Althusser insists that history is a process without a subject and argues that Marx's theoretical starting point was not "man" but the given mode of production or social formation. Marx and Engels actually write, in *The German Ideology*, "The premises from which we begin are not arbitrary ones, not dogmas, but real premises from which abstraction can only be made in the imagination. They are the real individuals, their activity and the material conditions under which they live."

Althusser treats the social relations of production as shaping the forces of production rather than the other way round, but if so, what determines the relations of production? Marx says:

> The fact is, therefore, that definite individuals who are productively active in a definite way enter into these definite social and political relations... The social structure and the state are continually evolving out of the life-process of definite individuals. (http://www.marxists.org/archive/marx/works/1845/german-ideology/ch01a.htm#a2)

Althusser says that people (with the exception of those able to achieve the level of "science") are trapped in ideology and even a fully communist society will not be able to dispense with ideology. *The Communist Manifesto* says that as a result of capitalism "man is at last compelled to face with sober senses his real conditions of life, and his relations with his kind".

In the matter of Ideological State Apparatuses, Althusser at least does not attribute his theory to Marx, but the theory is clearly "un-Marxist". The churches, the family, the trade unions and (all?) political parties may serve as channels for bourgeois ideology but they are clearly not *state* apparatuses and to present them as such is to greatly exaggerate the power of the capitalist state while, especially in the case of trade unions and workers' political parties, erasing the important contradiction between them and the state.

Even more important than Althusser's systematic misrepresentation of Marx's thought is what drove that misrepresentation – Stalinism. By Stalinism here I mean adherence to the whole tradition and set of political ideas which took over the international communist movement in the mid-1920s, the founding principles of which were the doctrine of "socialism in one country" (formulated by Stalin in 1924) and loyalty to the leadership of the Soviet Union. Khrushchev, for example, denounced the cult of personality of Stalin but remained, in this wider sense, a thoroughgoing Stalinist, as did Waldeck Rochet, Georges Marchais and the leaders of the PCF. And when I say Stalinism drove Althusser's misrepresentation of Marx I do not mean just that politically Althusser belonged to the Stalinist tradition (though he most certainly did) but that his whole system contained at its heart an attempt to forge a *philosophical* defence of Stalinism.

The original impetus behind his anti-humanism and his rejection of the concept of alienation was to defend Stalinism, both in Eastern Europe and internationally, against the critical deployment of these ideas, and it is worth noting that his downgrading of the early Marx was not that distant from the official Soviet view. Of great significance here is his claim, cited at the beginning of this section, that he was embarking on "the first left wing critique of Stalinism". This is an extraordinary claim. There is no evidence that Althusser ever seriously studied Trotsky but he could not possibly have been unaware of him. Moreover by the 1970s there were numerous left critiques of Stalinism, eg those of Serge, Céline, Dunayevskaya, James, Cliff, Deutscher, Mandel, Djilas, Marcuse, Fromm and the Frankfurt School, Lukács, Sartre, Kuron and Modzelewski (and many others). The implication of Althusser's claim, therefore, must be that all of these critiques, including and especially that of Trotsky, were right wing critiques – a repetition of the Stalinist line (and lie).

It is also the case, as we have seen (and as Gregory Elliott shows in detail), that Althusser's project was a half acknowledged philosophical accompaniment to Maoism, then exercising a considerable influence on the European left. Here it is important to understand that although Maoism deployed a much more radical rhetoric than Moscow or the Western Communist parties this was deceptive: it was not really a critique from the left. On the one hand Maoism *defended* Stalin and Stalinism against Khrushchev and enthusiastically supported the suppression of the Hungarian Revolution in 1956; on the other the Maoist regime in China was thoroughly Stalinist in terms of the complete absence of any workers' democracy, the absolute dictatorship of the party and the brutal pursuit of national capital accumulation (see, for example, N Harris, *The Mandate of Heaven: Marx and Mao in Modern China*, London, 1978). Unfortunately there is no sign that Althusser (like many European left intellectuals) ever looked seriously at what was actually happening on the ground in China, such as the mass starvation that accompanied the Great Leap Forward of 1958-61, as opposed to the declarations coming out of Beijing.

Althusser's attack on "economism" and his stress on the autonomy of different "levels" in any social formation enabled him to accommodate the idea that Stalin had made mistakes or even committed crimes without this reflecting anything fundamentally amiss in the "socialist" base of the Soviet Union. Similarly his downplaying of the primary role of the forces of production in relation to the relations of production in historical materialism dovetailed with the Maoist insistence that it was possible to achieve the transition to full communism in China despite its economic backwardness, ie its low level of productive forces. Later it also permitted Althusser to see Trotsky as essentially the same as Stalin because they both shared the economism of asserting the primacy of the productive forces.

In this respect Althusser shares a trait characteristic of much "academic" Marxism – the elevation of philosophical and methodological positions over social practice, of words over deeds. Never mind the river of blood that divided Trotskyism and Stalinism – the fact that Stalin and his cohorts were ensconced in the Kremlin while Trotsky was exiled and murdered and his supporters sent to the gulag, or the fact that they pursued opposed policies in every serious battle of the working class from 1923 onwards – the main thing is that they agreed (in words) about the primacy of the productive forces. Actually this is rampant philosophical idealism. For Althusser it permitted him to carry on talking about the PCF as if it were a revolutionary party when it had been pursuing a blatantly reformist practice for decades.

Overall Althusser's Stalinist structuralism produced a series of philosophical positions that reduced actual human beings ("men" in the language of the time) to mere "supports" or products of social structures and prisoners of ideology that gave them the illusion of being subjects without the potential to be so in reality. It thus restricted and diminished the project of working class revolutionary self-emancipation as the road to the liberation of all humanity.

It should also be said that Althusser's "theoretical practice" with its highly inflated, self-important language and terminology and its extreme anti-economism fitted like a glove the needs of a generation of left and "Marxist" academics in Britain in transition from the revolutionary hopes of 1968 to the disillusionment of the late 1970s and looking to build their careers. For many in this layer Althusserianism proved to be useful staging post on the road to poststructuralism, postmodernism and post-Marxism.

Finally, it is a vindication of one of the central themes of this book, namely the relationship between Marxist theory, revolutionary practice and working class struggle, that of our three major figures – Lukács, Gramsci and Althusser – the most useful philosophical contribution came from Gramsci, the revolutionary who had the closest involvement with actual workers in struggle, and the weakest from Althusser, who was most isolated and confined to the ivory tower.

13. The philosophy of practice

Writing in Mussolini's jail, Antonio Gramsci used to refer to Marxism as "the philosophy of practice" and he was right to do so. Marxism arises from the practice of the working class – it is a generalisation about world history from the standpoint of the activity/labour and struggle of the working class. Its aim is not just to interpret the world but guide the working class in its struggle to change it. All the core ideas of Marxist philosophy have real practical implications.

As Marx pointed out even crude 18th century materialism had clear socialist implications:

> There is no need for any great penetration to see...how necessarily materialism is connected with communism and socialism. If man draws all his knowledge, sensation, etc, from the world of the senses and the experience gained in it, then what has to be done is to arrange the empirical world in such a way that man experiences and becomes accustomed to what is truly human in it... If correctly understood interest is the principle of all morality, man's private interest must be made to coincide with the interest of humanity... If man is shaped by environment, his environment must be made human. If man is social by nature, he will develop his true nature only in society. (K Marx and F Engels, *The Holy Family*, in Marx, Engels, Lenin, *On Communist Society*, Moscow, 1978)

Moreover Marx and Engels's own non-mechanical materialism pointed to the fundamental role in human history, and therefore in action to shape history, of human labour and production. Similarly Marx's theory of alienation locates the root cause of alienation in people's loss of ownership and control of their own labour, and consequently of its products, and thus identifies the establishment of collective ownership and control of the conditions of production (by the working class) as the key to working class and human emancipation.

Dialectics has revolutionary implications because it is based on the fact that everything changes, and that therefore capitalism is doomed to perish. The materialist dialectic, says Marx:

> is a scandal and abomination to bourgeoisdom and its doctrinaire professors, because it includes in its comprehension and affirmative recognition of the existing state of things, at the same time also, the recognition of the negation of that state, of its inevitable breaking up; because it regards every historically developed social form as in fluid movement, and therefore takes into account its transient nature not less than its momentary existence; because it lets nothing impose upon it, and is in its essence critical and revolutionary. (K Marx, Afterword to the second German edition, *Capital*, Vol 1, as above, p29)

Dialectics, as Lenin showed in practice, is also extremely useful in the analysis of complex political situations and the development of revolutionary strategy and tactics.

Marx's theory of exploitation is not only an exposure of how the capitalists rob the workers and a key to grasping the laws of motion of capitalist production, but is also a pointer to the fundamental conflict of interest between capitalists and workers in every workplace and industry which has the practical implication that workers will organise to resist this exploitation (in trades unions etc) and that Marxists should support them in this.

The theory of exploitation also underpins the theory of class and class struggle which in turn is central to historical materialism. Historical materialism has generated numerous outstanding works of historical and social analysis but its main purpose is to understand the class struggle in the here and now and how the conflict between the forces and relations of production is leading to "an era of social revolution".

Marx's theory of the state, as a means of capitalist class rule which cannot be taken over and used by the working class, and of working class consciousness, dominated by the ideas of the ruling class but changing in struggle, both point directly to the need for revolution:

> Both for the production on a mass scale of this communist consciousness, and for the success of the cause itself, the alteration of men on a mass scale is necessary, an alteration which can only take place in a practical movement, a revolution; this revolution is necessary, therefore, not only because the ruling class cannot be overthrown in any other way, but also because the class overthrowing it can only in a revolution succeed in ridding itself of all the muck of ages and become fitted to found society anew. (K Marx and F Engels, *The German Ideology*, in D McLellan, ed, as above, p179)

The Marxist theory of morality, likewise, leads to the conclusion that the highest morality available to us in capitalist society is based on the needs and interests of the working class and its liberation.

In short all roads in Marxist philosophy, and Marxism as a whole, lead to the proletarian revolution. This raises the question as to what concretely and in practice can and should be done to bring about, and secure the victory of, this workers' revolution. And I mean by this what should *we* do, me the writer and you the reader, today, tomorrow and in the weeks, months and years ahead.

In the first place we should actively participate in the working class movement, in the trade unions, strikes, demonstrations, campaigns, meetings and so on that develop resistance to global capitalism, working always to raise the confidence and consciousness of working people and the oppressed. Secondly, in this process, we also have to build, in every country, revolutionary workers' parties.

There are a number of straightforward practical reasons why this is necessary. The capitalist class is highly centralised economically and politically by virtue of its control of state power. To defeat it the working class needs its own centralised political organisation – a political party. The ruling class exercises ideological hegemony over society by means of its control of the media, education and other institutions. The working class needs its own institutions of ideological struggle, to combat the influence of bourgeois ideas on the working class and within the workers' movement – it needs a party. Working class consciousness and confidence develops unevenly; the more conscious and committed workers need to organise themselves to fight for leadership in the workers' movement against the influence of the reformist trade union officials and labourite politicians who are already selling out and holding back the movement and will certainly betray it in a revolutionary situation. Again that means building a revolutionary party – one with roots in every workplace and community.

The revolutionary party is also a philosophical question and follows directly from many of the themes discussed in this book. Lukács called it "one of the most important intellectual questions of the revolution" (G Lukács, *History and Class Consciousness*, as above, p295). This is because it focuses on the dialectical relationship between objective circumstances and human intervention in the making of history. Revolutions are not made by revolutionaries. As Marx showed, they arise out of the objective contradictions in society when the existing relations of production have become a fetter on the development of the forces of production and they begin when the ongoing class struggle boils over. Revolution, the act of the working class itself, involves millions of hitherto dormant working people shaking off their passivity and moving into action on the streets and in their workplaces. Almost invariably this starts spontaneously and arises from a long and gradual accumulation of anger, bitterness and frustration in the hearts and minds of working people suddenly exploding in collective defiance (in dialectical terms a transformation of quantity into quality). No leadership can order this or force it into being. From the standpoint of revolutionaries, necessarily a minority within the working class in "normal" circumstances, the outbreak of revolution is an objective condition which can be encouraged and prepared for but not ordained.

However, if revolutions begin spontaneously that is not how they end. Revolutions are a process lasting months or even years after the initial entry of the masses onto the stage of history. In the course of those months and years the struggle ebbs and flows, the working class moves forward, is forced back and moves forward again, all the while learning political lessons and clarifying its ideas. If, in this period, the conscious revolutionary socialists lack a party or are weakly organised they are likely to be swept along by enthusiastic moods among the masses or fall into voluntarist illusions that they can make the revolution by their own will power. This can lead to premature attempts to seize power which are easily crushed.

For the revolution to be brought to a victorious conclusion it must first pass through a period or moment when the balance of power between the classes is more or less even. Trotsky, referring to Germany just before Hitler came to power, compared such a situation to "a ball on top of a pyramid [which] the slightest impact can cause to roll down to left or the right" (L Trotsky, *The Struggle Against Fascism in Germany*, New York, 1971, p137). In this situation, the role of the revolutionary party and its ability to take the initiative, always important, becomes decisive. It makes the difference between victory and defeat. And at such a moment any tendency to mechanical determinism or fatalism is likely to be disastrous, in that it will be likely to allow the revolutionary crisis to slip by.

Up to now the nearest the working class has come to the overthrow of capitalism internationally is the revolutionary wave of 1917-23 that grew out of the First World War. The two most important revolutions in that process were the Russian Revolution and the German Revolution, the former victorious (until the Stalinist counter-revolution in the 1920s) and the latter defeated. Both these revolutions passed through the phases discussed above. Both began spontaneously – the Russian in February 1917 and the German in November 1918 – and both brought down their respective emperors in a few days. In both there were attempts at premature insurrection – in Petrograd in July 1917 and in Germany in January 1919 – and in both there were successfully resisted right-wing coups – in Russia, the Kornilov revolt at the end of August 1917 and, in Germany, the Kapp Putsch in March 1920. In both there came a decisive moment – October 1917 in Russia, October 1923 in Germany – when a majority of the working class supported taking power. But whereas in Russia the Bolsheviks led by Lenin were able to prevent a full-scale confrontation in July and live to fight another day, in Germany the young Spartacus League was caught up in the 1919 rising and its outstanding leaders, Rosa Luxemburg and Karl Liebknecht, were murdered. Then in October the Russian workers, under the leadership of Lenin, Trotsky and the Bolsheviks, were able to establish soviet power, whereas in Germany in 1923 the leadership of the German Communist Party sat on their hands and let the moment pass.

What made the difference? It cannot be attributed to "objective" or sociological factors. Objectively Germany was far more ready for socialism than Russia and had a much larger, more powerful and better organised working class. Moreover the economic and social crisis in Germany was even more severe than in Russia – this was a time of extreme hyperinflation with workers carrying their wages home in wheelbarrows. What made the difference was the quality of revolutionary leadership. The Bolshevik Party entered the February Revolution with about 26,000 members and 14 years of strategic and tactical training in a wide variety of different and complex stages of the struggle. The Spartacus League, by contrast, was much smaller, much less experienced and much more loosely organised; consequently it swung between voluntaristic ultra-left errors (like boycotting elections) and fatalistic passivity.

This is why Trotsky, analysing the failure of the German Revolution, wrote:

> Bolshevism is not a doctrine (ie not merely a doctrine) but a system of revolutionary training for the proletarian uprising. What is the Bolshevisation of Communist Parties? It is giving them such a training, and effecting such a selection of the leading staff, as would prevent them from drifting when the hour for their October strikes. "That is the whole Hegel, and the wisdom of books and the meaning of all philosophy..." (L Trotsky, "The Lessons of October", in *The Challenge of the Left Opposition (1923-25)*, New

York, 1975, p256. For a full account of the German disaster see C Harman, *The Lost Revolution: Germany 1918-23*, London, 1982.)

Since the defeat of the German Revolution the working class has risen against the system on many occasions – China 1925-27, Spain 1936, Italy and Greece at the end of the Second World War, Hungary 1956, France 1968, Portugal 1974-75 among others – but has not yet succeeded in achieving a breakthrough. The absence of revolutionary parties of sufficient strength, not the inability or unwillingness of the working class to fight, is the main explanation for this repeated failure.

The crisis facing humanity is now extremely dangerous. Not only are we in the worst economic crisis since the 1930s, with our rulers internationally determined to make working people pay the price, but there is the looming threat of catastrophic and runaway climate change which will produce almost unimaginable suffering for billions of people. These twin crises will generate immense resistance and upheavals. The building internationally of mass revolutionary parties in and of the working class is the main thing we can do to help bring about a positive outcome to this titanic struggle.

This is the principal practical conclusion that flows from Marxist philosophy. At the same time it is clear that the construction of these revolutionary parties requires at its heart a materialist and dialectical grasp of how society works and how history is made – Marxist philosophy.

Appendix
Hardt, Negri, Standing and Žižek: the working class revisited

The onset of global economic crisis and the recent international wave of struggle has thrown up, across Europe and North America, a new generation of activists. Among many of these activists the dominant set of ideas is what can be described as "soft autonomism" – a not very clearly defined semi-anarchism committed to direct democracy in mass assemblies and often sceptical of, or even hostile to, traditional trade unionism and labour movement political parties, including would-be revolutionary parties. Corresponding to this spontaneous mood and at the same time helping to shape it have been a number of intellectual figures, of whom Michael Hardt and Antonio Negri are among the most important.

Negri is a political philosopher who came from a Marxist (Stalinist) background with the Italian Communist Party, and moved to radical autonomism in the late 1960s and 1970s, via the far-left party Potere Operaio (Workers' Power), which focused heavily on workplace struggle. As an autonomist he theorised the idea of "the refusal of work" as a revolutionary strategy in opposition to employed workers who were seen as having bought into the system. Falsely accused of involvement in left wing "terrorist" group the Red Brigades, Negri spent a number of years in prison. He is now best known for his co-authorship with the American literary theorist Michael Hardt of a number of books, the most influential of which are *Empire* (2000) and *Multitude* (2004). For Hardt and Negri "Empire" is a new world order which has replaced, or is replacing, the "imperialism" of classical Marxism. It is an overarching network of economic, social and political power, roughly corresponding to the multinational corporations and the world market, which transcends and is increasingly independent of nation-states.

Empire, they argue, "stands clearly over the multitude and subjects it to the rule of its overarching machine", but from another perspective:

> the hierarchy is reversed. The multitude is the real productive force of our social world, whereas Empire is a mere apparatus of capture that lives off the vitality of the multitude – as Marx would say, a vampire regime of accumulated dead labour that survives only by sucking of the blood of the living. (M Hardt and A Negri, *Empire*, Cambridge MA, 2000, p62)

In this schema the multitude is posited as the new social (revolutionary) subject, replacing "the people", "the masses" and Marx's "working class". The multitude is distinguished from the people and the masses in that, "The people has traditionally been a unitary conception," which "reduces diversity to a unity and makes of the population a single identity" and "all differences are submerged and drowned in the masses. All the colours of the population fade to grey":

> The multitude, in contrast, is many...different cultures, races, ethnicities, genders, and sexual orientations; different forms of labour; different ways of living; different views of the world; and different desires... In the multitude social differences remain different. The multitude is many coloured, like Joseph's magical coat. (M Hardt and A Negri, *Multitude*, London, 2004, pxiv)

The multitude is distinguished from the working class because:

> The concept of the working class has come to be used as an exclusive concept...to refer only to industrial workers, separating them from workers in agriculture, services and other sectors...[or] to all waged workers, separating them from the poor, unpaid domestic labourers, and all others who do not receive a wage. The multitude, in contrast is an open inclusive concept. (as above, ppxiv-xv.)

The appeal of this concept is clear. It presses all the buttons of the "common sense" of a newly radicalising young generation who have grown up with and developed a mixture of postmodern identity politics and liberal individualism (absorbed from neoliberalism) and also been subjected to a pretty relentless critique of the concept of class in general (as divisive) and of the working class in particular (as outmoded). Notice how it references buzzwords such as "exclusion" and "inclusion" and nods discreetly in the direction of the kitsch Lloyd Webber musical. They even say "the internet is a good initial image or model for the multitude" (as above, pxv).

Notice also that the argument is developed more in terms of concepts than in terms of material social relations and proceeds by assertion rather than evidence. Consequently it would be just as possible and plausible to say, "all differences are submerged and drowned in the multitude", or "the working class is many different cultures, races, ethnicities, genders and sexual orientations, etc".

But if its appeal is obvious this doesn't prevent "the multitude" as a substitute for "the working class" being a flawed concept. This is because "the multitude" in its open inclusiveness masks and erases real social differences which it is essential for any serious strategy for revolution to take account of. In the first place it erases real differences of interest between proletarians and petty bourgeois who are small-scale employers (and exploiters) or middle class managers who are agents of capital. This is not to say there cannot be an alliance between the working class and sections of the petty bourgeoisie or middle class but it must be an alliance not a merger and it matters who exercises political hegemony (as Gramsci would have put it). The petty bourgeoisie is not inherently a socialist/collectivist class. It can be led in a socialist direction by the working class and this will strengthen the struggle, as when local shopkeepers support a strike, but if the petty bourgeoisie or managers lead the workers the direction will most likely be reactionary or even fascist.

In the second place it obscures differences of social power. Students, the unemployed and peasants all have important parts to play in the struggle for socialism – and no serious Marxist has ever thought of excluding them – but they do not have the same power, the same social weight, as employed workers, especially workers in large workplaces and huge cities. This is because the latter have the power to stop production and hit the bosses' profits in a way that the former do not. This is a strategic not a moral judgement and not about "privileging" workers. It is akin to understanding that in street fighting with the police the leading role is likely to be played by fit youngsters not pensioners (like me) who can't run, or that soldiers in a tank have more power than soldiers on foot.

On 15 February 2003 in London the "multitude" marched against the Iraq war, all 2 million of us, but Blair took no notice. Had the mass demonstration been combined with large-scale strike action which put the bourgeoisie under pressure economically and threatened a much deeper social crisis it would have been much harder for Blair to press ahead. Similarly in the Egyptian Revolution of 2011 Mubarak continued to cling to power in the face of gigantic street mobilisations but was forced out when these were complemented by large-scale strikes. The multitude can occupy squares but workers can occupy workplaces. Occupied workplaces are our side's "tanks". Workers' councils have to be based (though not exclusively) on workplaces; this is the key to both their power and their democracy (the ability to exercise the right of recall etc).

However, there is more involved here than these strategic considerations. The concept of the working class is a cornerstone of Marxist theory and philosophy. Remove this cornerstone and the whole house starts to collapse. Without the concept of the working class the theory of alienation, which is focused on alienated labour (as opposed to psychological and idealist theories), falls apart. Without the working class the labour theory of value and surplus value (ie of exploitation) unravels, followed rapidly by the whole argument of *Capital* down to the tendency of the rate of profit to decline. The concept of the working class is a key part of the whole theory of class struggle which is at the heart of historical materialism. Remove the working class and it is necessary to reconstruct historical materialism as a whole. Materialist dialectics is a development of philosophy made from the vantage point of the working class, and with the historical emergence of the working class as its social base.

Marxism is a remarkably integrated and coherent worldview. Its component parts – its philosophy, theory of history, economics, sociology and politics – interlock and complement one another. It derives this coherence, not from the system-creating genius of Marx (who never actually set out such a system), but from being the world viewed from a new vantage point, the standpoint of the working class. This emphatically does not mean Marxism does not need to be developed on all fronts in order to keep up with an ever changing reality, but the working class is the foundation and if that is pulled away the whole theory has to be rebuilt. It is not possible to remove the working class and insert some other agency in its place – the Red Army (à la Stalin), the peasantry (a la Mao), the guerrilla band (à la Castro), the marginalised (Marcuse), the party or terrorist group on behalf of the working class, or the multitude or the precariat – and leave the rest of Marxism intact.

To their credit Hardt and Negri would seem to realise this, hence their attempt, in *Empire*, to create a new general theory of the system in place of Marx's *Capital*, Lenin's and Bukharin's studies of imperialism (which rested on *Capital*) and so on. But leaving aside that *Empire* is not remotely in the same league as *Capital* as a scientific work, this attempt failed almost at the first hurdle. Central to *Empire* was the claim that this new order of power was escaping dependence on the nation-state. This theory, always mistaken, was manifestly confounded by the Afghan and Iraq wars and the crisis of 2008 with its accompanying massive state interventions to save the banks. Politically they retreat (though it is ambiguous) from socialism to democracy as "the project of the multitude" (see *Multitude*, as above, pxi and throughout) and philosophically Negri retreated from Marx, via Althusser's anti-humanism, all the way to Spinoza – a philosopher of the early development of capitalism.

Guy Standing has proposed a different alternative to the working class: "the precariat". He writes, "Every progressive political movement has been built on the anger, needs and aspirations of the emerging major class. Today that class is the precariat." For Standing this is "a new dangerous class...a class in the making" which consists of a "multitude of insecure people...in and out of jobs, including millions of frustrated educated youth" (http://www.policynetwork.net/pno_detail.aspx?ID=4004&title=+The+Precariat+%E2%80%93+The+new+dangerous+class).

Again the appeal of this concept as a description is obvious for there are millions who live such precarious lives but this does not make it a valid theory. Standing is an economist not a philosopher and his approach is empirical. There is a major debate about the facts (see for example K Doogan, *New Capitalism? The Transformation of Work*, London, 2009). There is no space to debate these details here but there are basic weaknesses in Standing's conception.

Every designation of a particular class only makes sense in relation to other classes in the structure of society and for Standing the overall structure, nationally and internationally, is as follows: at the top a small class of super-rich or plutocrats; below them a "salariat" with secure full-time employment and below them the precariat. This model is flawed because it unites, in the salariat, groups that have very different interests – eg senior managers, university vice chancellors, hospital consultants, etc, and nurses, teachers, social workers and skilled factory workers, etc – namely middle class managers and white collar and skilled industrial workers. It also divides those who need to be united, ie those same white collar and blue collar workers from temporary, insecure workers and the unemployed.

Also Standing errs in making "precarity", which was always *one aspect* of the proletarian condition, extensively described by Marx in both the *Communist Manifesto* and *Capital*, into the essential determinant of class, and in separating one part of the working class, the precarious workers, from the class as a whole. As with the multitude the question of power is crucial here – precarious workers have less power than regularly employed workers and not enough power by themselves, especially if set against employed workers, to overthrow capitalism or free themselves. So once again what starts as an apparent simple insertion – precariat for proletariat – requiring new tactics and strategy, rapidly unravels the whole theory and the whole project. In Standing's case the project becomes not the revolution or the socialist transformation of society but the revival of social democracy on the basis of "representing" the precariat and achieving reforms on its behalf, as he believes it did for the industrial working class in the past.

Finally there is the instance of the popular "philosopher guru", Slavoj Žižek. There is a widespread fashion, encouraged by the media, for inventing new social class categories on the basis of surface impressions. Žižek was unable to resist this temptation in a recent article in the *London Review of Books* (Slavoj Žižek, "The Revolt of the Salaried Bourgeoisie", *London Review of Books*, 26 January 2012). It is another good example of the theoretical confusion this leads to. Žižek argues that the capitalist class proper is disappearing and being replaced by a "salaried bourgeoisie" who receive "surplus wages" which are "rather more than the proletarian 'minimum wage'" and he then extends this class, rather like Standing's "salariat" (and indeed Max Weber's educated middle class) to include "administrators, public servants, doctors, lawyers, journalists, intellectuals and artists" and crucially, "those privileged workers who have guaranteed jobs (teachers, public transport workers, police)" and also "students" whose motivation is "fear that higher education will no longer guarantee them a surplus wage in later life".

He then argues that the recent mass strikes and protests (the 30 November 2011 mass strike in Britain, etc) are a revolt of this salaried bourgeoisie:

> In times of crisis, the obvious candidates for "belt-tightening" are the lower levels of the salaried bourgeoisie: political protest is their only recourse if they are to avoid joining the proletariat. Although their protests are nominally directed against the brutal logic of the market, they are in effect protesting about

the gradual erosion of their (politically) privileged economic place...driven by fear of losing their surplus wage. These are not proletarian protests, but protests against the threat of being reduced to proletarians. Who dares strike today, when having a permanent job is itself a privilege? Not low-paid workers in (what remains of) the textile industry etc but those privileged workers who have guaranteed jobs (teachers, public transport workers, police). (S Žižek, "The Revolt of the Salaried Bourgeoisie", as above, p10)

Clearly if transport workers and teachers and public sector workers with permanent jobs are all "salaried bourgeoisie" then precious little is left of the working class or its struggle. And this is not just a question of Britain. Teachers and public transport workers along with tax collectors have all undertaken major strikes in Egypt and played an important role in the developing Egyptian Revolution. But then Žižek is also inclined to see that extraordinary struggle and the numerous general strikes in Greece as revolts of his "salaried bourgeoisie". If this is the case the Marxist perspective of workers' revolution is completely undermined.

What all these examples illustrate and reinforce is the centrality and indispensability of the concept of the working class or proletariat for Marxist theory and philosophy as a whole. Marxism is the theory of proletarian revolution. You can't have one without the other.

A guide to further reading

There is a vast literature on Marxist philosophy. Here are some suggestions for exploring the subject further. Almost every aspect of Marxist philosophy is controversial and my inclusion of a work here signifies that I think it is important or useful, not that I agree with it.

General introductions to Marxism

Chris Harman, *How Marxism Works* (Bookmarks, 1997), http://marxists.org/archive/harman/1979/marxism/

Alex Callinicos, *The Revolutionary Ideas of Karl Marx* (Bookmarks, 2010).

Kieran Allen, *Marx and the Alternative to Capitalism* (Pluto, 2011).

John Molyneux, *What is the Real Marxist Tradition?* (Haymarket, 2003), http://www.marxisme.dk/arkiv/molyneux/realmarx/index.htm

By Marx and Engels

The Collected Works of Marx and Engels plus many other key Marxist writings are available online at the Marxist Internet Archive (http://www.marxists.org). References here are to the archive but various print editions are also available.

Karl Marx, *Economic and Philosophic Manuscripts of 1844*, http://www.marxists.org/archive/marx/works/1844/manuscripts/preface.htm

Karl Marx and Frederick Engels, *The German Ideology*,

http://www.marxists.org/archive/marx/works/1845/german-ideology/

Karl Marx and Frederick Engels, *The Communist Manifesto*, http://www.marxists.org/archive/marx/works/1848/communist-manifesto/

Karl Marx, Preface to *A Contribution to the Critique of Political Economy*, http://www.marxists.org/archive/marx/works/1859/critique-pol-economy/preface.htm

Frederick Engels, *Anti-Dühring*, http://www.marxists.org/archive/marx/works/1877/anti-Dühring/index.htm

Frederick Engels, *Ludwig Feuerbach and the End of Classical German Philosophy*, http://www.marxists.org/archive/marx/works/1886/ludwig-feuerbach/index.htm

Karl Marx, "Theses on Feuerbach", http://www.marxists.org/archive/marx/works/1845/theses/theses.htm

Frederick Engels, *The Dialectics of Nature*, http://www.marxists.org/archive/marx/works/1883/don/index.htm

Some other classic Marxist texts

V I Lenin, *Collected Works*, Vol 38: Philosophical Notebooks, http://www.marxists.org/archive/lenin/works/cw/volume38.htm

Leon Trotsky, *In Defence of Marxism*, http://www.marxists.org/archive/trotsky/idom/dm/index.htm

Trotsky's Notebooks, 1933-35: Writings on Lenin, Dialectics and Evolutionism (Columbia University Press, 1986).

Georg Lukács, *History and Class Consciousness*, http://www.marxists.org/archive/Lukács/works/history/index.htm

Antonio Gramsci, *Prison Notebooks: Selections* (Lawrence and Wishart, 1998).

Other general works on Marxist philosophy

John Rees, *The Algebra of Revolution* (Routledge, 1998).
Raya Dunayevskaya, *Marxism and Freedom* (Humanity Books, 2000).
Herbert Marcuse, *Reason and Revolution* (Routledge & Keegan Paul, 1968), http://www.marxists.org/reference/archive/marcuse/works/reason/index.htm (incomplete).
Helena Sheehan, *Marxism and the Philosophy of Science* (Humanities Press International, 1993).

On alienation

Dan Swain, *Alienation: An Introduction to Marx's Theory* (Bookmarks, 2012).
István Mészáros, *Marx's Theory of Alienation* (Merlin, 1975)
Bertell Ollman, *Alienation: Marx's Conception of Man in Capitalist Society* (Cambridge University Press, 1971).

On historical materialism

Chris Harman, *Marxism and History* (Bookmarks, 1998) contains essays on "Base and Superstructure" and "From Feudalism to Capitalism".
Paul Blackledge, *Reflections on the Marxist Theory of History* (Manchester University Press, 2006).
Alex Callinicos, *Making History* (Polity Press, 1989).
Chris Harman, *A People's History of the World* (Verso, 2008).

On human nature

John Molyneux, *Is Human Nature a Barrier to Socialism?* (Socialist Worker, 1993).
Norman Geras, *Marx and Human Nature: Refutation of a Legend* (Verso, 1983).

On determinism

John Molyneux, "Is Marxism deterministic?", *International Socialism* 68 (autumn 1995), http://www.marxists.org/history/etol/writers/molyneux/1995/xx/determin.htm

On religion

Karl Marx, *Introduction to A Critique of Hegel's Philosophy of Right*, http://www.marxists.org/archive/marx/works/1843/ critique-hpr/intro.htm
Karl Marx and Frederick Engels, *On Religion*, http://www.marxists.org/archive/marx/works/subject/religion/index.htm
John Molyneux, "More than Opium: Marxism and Religion", *International Socialism* 119 (summer 2008), http://www.isj.org.uk/index.php4?id=456&issue=119
Paul N Siegel, *The Meek and the Militant* (Zed Books, 1989).
Chris Harman, "The Prophet and the Proletariat", *International Socialism* 64 (autumn 1994), http://www.marxists.org/archive/harman/1994/xx/islam.htm

On morality and justice

Leon Trotsky, *Their Morals and Ours*, http://www.marxists.org/archive/trotsky/1938/morals/morals.htm

Alex Callinicos, *The Resources of Critique* (Polity Press, 2006).

Paul Blackledge, "Marxism and Ethics", *International Socialism* 120 (autumn 2008), http://www.isj.org.uk/index.php4?id=486&issue=120

Norman Geras, "The Controversy about Marx and Justice", *New Left Review* I/150 (March-April 1985).

Steven Lukes, *Marxism and Morality* (Oxford University Press, 1987).

On Engels

Lindsey German, Chris Harman, Paul McGarr, John Rees, "The Revolutionary Ideas of Frederick Engels", *International Socialism* 65 (special issue, 1994), http://www.marxists.de/theory/engels/index.htm

On Althusser and Gramsci

Gregory Elliott, *Althusser: the Detour of Theory* (Haymarket, 2009).

Chris Harman, "Philosophy and Revolution", *International Socialism* 21 (autumn 1983), http://www.marxists.org/archive/harman/1983/xx/phil-rev.html

Chris Harman, "The Emperor has no Clothes", *International Socialism* 125 (winter 2010), http://www.marxists.org/archive/harman/2010/xx/emperor.htm

Peter D Thomas, *The Gramscian Moment* (Haymarket, 2011).

Chris Harman, "Gramsci, the Prison Notebooks and Philosophy", *International Socialism* 114 (spring 2007), http://www.marxists.org/archive/harman/2007/xx/prisnbooks.htm

On Negri

Alex Callinicos, "Toni Negri in perspective", *International Socialism* 92 (autumn 2001).